TACKLE C

TACKLE CRICKET

COLIN COWDREY
Kent and England

STANLEY PAUL
London

STANLEY PAUL & CO. LTD
3 Fitzroy Square, London W1

An imprint of the Hutchinson Publishing Group

London Melbourne Sydney Auckland
Wellington Johannesburg Cape Town
and agencies throughout the world

First published 1964
Second impression April 1969
This edition May 1974

Printed in Great Britain by The Anchor Press Ltd,
and bound by Wm. Brendon & Son Ltd,
both of Tiptree, Essex

ISBN 0 09 120670 7

0 09 120671 5

CONTENTS

ILLUSTRATIONS

The author acknowledges Patrick Eagar for
permission to reproduce the photographs of
which he owns the copyright.

INTRODUCTION

So, then, you have caught the cricket bug! Well, you have come to the right person, because I have had it for thirty-five years and you and I are just two of the millions down the years, from every walk of life, and of all ages, who have become captivated by this summer game, which is peculiar to England and Englishmen.

There are three distinct aspects of the game of cricket, I suppose. First, the rather dull matter of the laws, which have to be understood; although I think it is true to say there are few top-class cricketers who bother themselves with them, but at least they have to have a working knowledge of them. Second, there is the technical side of the game, which has more than its fair share of coverage in every cricket library. Third, there is the task of putting one's technical knowledge into action out in the middle.

Come with me through these pages whilst I discuss the technical side of the game, and I will try to help you relate it to your own game. You must not accept all I have to say blindly, but rather I beseech you to sift out for yourself those grains which most suit you.

There are so many types of cricketer that in generalizing it is difficult to speak for any one particular group. There is the man with a wonderful eye and all the natural attributes to make the outstanding athlete. To him the half-volley cries out to be hit in the most natural way. There is the useful all-round games player, with a certain eye and sense of co-ordination, who has to attain technical correctness to achieve any degree of consistency. Then there is the third type who not blest with a very good eye and plays some terribly risky, rustic strokes. He is never able to attain consistency, but is so completely dedicated and devoted to this game of cricket that he goes on and on, hoping to achieve the impossible. These are the ones I feel for most of all.

Although most of the top-class players observe basic principles to a certain extent, with experience and constant practice they have developed certain unorthodox methods of their own improvisation. These are confusing to a young player. The experts become increasingly confident and extremely successful with these methods as they grow to recognize the strengths and weaknesses of each particular stroke. The danger comes when youngsters try to imitate these strokes without knowing the pitfalls which surround them. I am thinking of the Denis Compton sweep or the Bradman pull or the Peter May hit, wide of mid-on, or the Barry Richards square cut or the Garfield Sobers cover drive standing absolutely still. All these strokes are peculiar to the maestros, strokes not to be thought of, then, until the budding player has achieved a certain framework of his own.

So, whoever you are, then, join me as I think around the basic problems. Try to grapple with them, try to understand them, try to apply them to your own game, and then, and not until then, move towards developing your own natural style.

I

BATTING

STRENGTH—brute-force strength, of course—is of great assistance, but it is really the combination of a sharp eye, strong wrists and this mysterious thing called 'ball sense' which comprise the ingredients of a good player. There are three distinct stages in the maturing of the top-class batsman.

As a youngster he must be encouraged to hit the ball in a natural and uninhibited way. There is nothing more depressing than seeing a youngster between six and eleven being forced by an over-indulgent father to play the stiff, defensive strokes to a pattern. His natural method will be to deposit each ball to cowshot corner. The air shot is a sorry sight and the onlookers will be tempted to chide 'Play straight'. But first he must be encouraged to hit the ball really hard and to know the feel of the ball in the middle of the bat.

Every now and again the mild suggestion to hit the ball straight back at the bowler, or, better still, over the bowler's head, will serve as a challenge, and before very long the straighter hit, when successfully achieved, will provide more of a thrill than the cowshot.

After a while it is clear that the youngster is never going to lose the knack of hitting the ball truly hard and often, and then is the time to think of grooving an orthodox swing of the bat. After all, by this stage you are looking for him to make a few runs in the middle; in other words, you are expecting him to build an innings.

Building an innings requires a tight defence. It is not sufficient to be able to play every scoring stroke in the book, when the first good-length straight ball knocks the middle stump out of the ground. The process of building a defence is dull but vital. While this defence-building is going on the attacking side must always be kept going. Never allow a boy to practise so hard on defence through several practice sessions without setting aside a few moments each time for hitting the ball with gay abandon.

Whilst the defence is being crystallized, and the attacking shots are developing, the mental approach becomes all-important. This is not merely a matter of temperament alone but the intelligence to know which strokes to employ against any particular bowler under certain conditions and against the different field settings. This can only be attained the hard way—by learning from mistakes—and there is no short cut to such experience. Come to the nets with me and establish the basic principles.

The Grip

Well, there's the bat on the ground, face downwards. Stand upright and to attention, but instead of putting the palms of your hands down the sides of your legs, fingers pointing to the ground in the normal way, turn both hands up, fingers pointing straight ahead of you with palms facing flat to the ground. Bend down, put both palms on to the handle of the bat and pick up the bat without stopping to think further. You will find that with a slight adjustment of the fingers for comfort you have found the most orthodox grip.

Ideally you should hold the bat with your hands close together and as near the top of the handle as you can. At the start of an innings it is helpful to separate the hands, with the bottom hand as low as you like. At such times everyone is nervous, and it is well worth spending a few minutes playing yourself in. It is a good thing to restrict your back-lift, allowing the bottom hand to become dominant, guiding the bat down the line of the ball in a defensive role. This should not prevent you from stroking the full toss or long hop away for runs. As your confidence gathers, so this bottom hand can creep up the bat to the right position for the full swing of the stroke.

The exception to prove the rule is Basil d'Oliviera, whose bottom hand is always very low down. No one can time the ball better or hit the ball farther than d'Oliviera, and yet the fingers of his right hand usually rest along the shoulder of the bat. Just one tip, which is my personal view. Remember to grip the bat as tightly as you can in the top hand, feeling all the flesh in the palm of your hand squeezing the top of the handle, at the same time relaxing the right hand so completely that the bat is held lightly in the fingers. You will find that when the time comes for you to call for power the strength will come at the right moment and you will have achieved a better measure of timing. Make a point of trying this during your next net practice. You will be surprised at the difference it makes.

The Stance

Stand, then, at the wicket in an easy, relaxed way, with the heels six to nine inches apart and both feet parallel to the crease, the weight equally balanced but taken on the front part of the feet. The knees should be relaxed and slightly bent, and although there should be no movement of the feet until the length of the ball is judged, I think one should be conscious of a certain movement within one's feet, a complete transference of weight from the heels on to the toes, making for a springiness, ready to move in any direction you want.

But first it is best to keep the front shoulder pointed at the bowler, the other shoulder hidden from view, your head turned square to the bowler, peering at him round your front shoulder. This is the perfect way of playing against bowlers who bowl at your off-stump and outside. If the bowling is directed at the leg stump, or down the leg side, this orthodox stance does not lend itself to fluent on-side play. It is much better to open up slightly. The left toe should point to mid-off, the left shoulder to mid-on and the other shoulder will come round into view. This will prevent cramping of the leg-side strokes.

The Back-lift

The back-lift is always rather a thorn in the coach's flesh. He will try to persuade his young protégé to pick the bat up straight, or even to first slip at the very extreme, knowing only too well that so many of the great players do not adhere to this. It is not essential, then, but I think it is much better to start with the idea that you are going to pick up the bat straight to ensure that it comes down straight. It is difficult for the young batsman to bring the bat in again straight or hit through on to the off-side once the back-lift has begun crooked. For this reason I insist that the bat be taken back over the off-stump so that the full range of orthodox strokes are at your command. As you mature and your strokes develop, then is the time to experiment. This may result in you finding it unnecessary to be quite so rigid in keeping the back-lift straight. For myself, I try to pick the bat up over the off-stump.

Keep the Head Still

If I have to point to any one thing which is of prime importance it is the position of the head in every stroke. I cannot over-emphasize the value of keeping the head absolutely upright, turned towards the bowler, with both eyes as level as possible. In every stroke the head should maintain one solid position, never falling to one side. It may sound trite, but if the head is still, there is an even chance of a firm and well-timed stroke.

If you were to take a slow-motion film of all the great players I think one would be very struck by the position of the head in all their strokes. When I am playing badly I go to a net and make myself relax everything else, but keep my head still and eye level, and make a point of achieving this in all my strokes. Speaking for my own game, this is one of the most forgotten and least emphasized tenets of good batsmanship. I recommend it to all.

Let me sum up:

1. Grip which feels comfortable, very tight with the top hand, a relaxed bottom hand.
2. Stance, with feet wide enough apart to establish a good balance, weight thrown from heels on to toes.
3. Front shoulder pointing to the bowler, back shoulder obscured.
4. A back-lift which is as straight as comfortable.
5. Head still.

Now we can start to think about the two basic strokes—forward and back, whether it be defence or attack.

Forward and Back

Upon the forward stroke and the back stroke rests the whole framework of batsmanship, and from these two positions comes the complete range of stroke play. I will try to analyse the art of batsmanship, as I have tried to do in my own particular game.

Now, the first and most complicated thing for the youngster to grapple with is the determination of the length of the ball. I remember asking all and sundry, as a youngster, 'When should I play forward and when should I play back?' When aged ten I was in this stage of indecision and remember being taken to a first-class match and setting out to watch Len Hutton very carefully. I scrutinized every movement in the hope that I would decipher the reasons which prompted him to play forward or back. I had assumed that if I was observant, half an hour's homework—which I knew to be the limit of my concentration—would provide the answer. I never expected to be sent home in more of a maze than ever before. The reason for this, as I was to discover in later years, lay in the fact that above a certain standard on good, true, reliable wickets it does not really make any difference to the great player—he can play forward or back at any time. For instance, the great player can play forward to a ball short of a length, or even shorter, and as it rises up so he can steer it down through the gully or through the short legs. Just as easily, the great player can play back to a half-volley or full toss. Because they know how to achieve the perfect balance and subtle timing they can drive the ball through the covers or straight back past the bowler for four with all the power in the world. So then, like the foreigner trying to grapple with the vagaries of the English language, famous for its inconsistency, the youngster is not necessarily going to have his query settled by watching the great player going through the motions.

Let me try to reduce the problem to its simplest terms. I believe that you should aim to play forward as much as possible. What would happen if every ball bowled were met

Geoffrey Boycott completes a cover drive and hopes to find the gap in the field. Note the head in the perfect position and weight transferred through the ball onto the front foot.

Asif Iqbal pushes the ball into the covers, scents the opportunity
for a quick single, he calls and springs into action. This is an
art in itself and brings joy to batting.

by a left foot thrust down the wicket? Now, if the ball is a full toss, or well pitched up, there is no problem and the stroke is played quite comfortably.

If the ball is pitched three to four feet short of your front foot at full stretch you can still play through the ball quite freely, with a straight, defensive bat—again, no problem. Anything pitched shorter still of this length, say two yards or more short of this front foot, you will soon find causes considerable discomfort. I believe, then, by playing forward to every ball bowled during one practice session you can soon teach yourself which is the awkward rising ball that needs a back stroke. After all, this awkward delivery, pitching nine feet short of your front foot at full stretch, cries out for you to move back into the stumps in order to give yourself more time to see the ball off the pitch. Here, then, lies the crux of the problem.

Any ball which pitches in this little area between your front foot and two yards away one can deal with very effectively on the forward stroke. Then there comes a definite line between six to nine feet, a distinct area of no-man's-land which is your blind spot. This is the vulnerable length which the bowler is seeking to find as often as possible. It is a narrow line, no more than three feet wide (in the case of a slow or medium pace bowler), where it is impossible to say whether it is best to play forward or back. 'When in doubt, play forward', and it is a good rule to remember, but when the ball pitches short of that very narrow line, nine feet or more away from your front foot at full stretch, then is the time to play back.

So, then, to all those who are grappling with this problem I would urge them to devote one practice session to testing my theory. Play forward to everything for a few overs. Look out for full toss on the one hand and long hop at the other

B

end of the scale. In between there is going to be a narrow area of no-man's-land where you are going to be in doubt. If you have these three distinct areas in mind you will soon be able to teach yourself which length of delivery demands back play or forward play.

Until you mature into the higher grades of cricket it is vital that you learn this as soon as possible. It is only when you have become an established player and know the consequences of breaking the orthodox rules that it is safe to vary. Certainly you must not be too much influenced by watching the top-class player with regard to this particular aspect of the game.

Let's Bat

Imagine that you are standing at the wicket and have a moment or two to think while the bowler is walking back. You are just about to start an innings. Do you just stand there with a blank expression on your face, which only shelters a vacant mind?—if so, I must put an end to that. It is a good thing to be relaxed, of course, but you must be armed with positive ideas. Apart from anything else, this breeds concentration. You must approach an innings with a clear insight into your own armoury. I like to simplify things to straight back-lift and my two strokes, forward and back.

Here is my foundation, which is unalterable and clear-cut—the right stance, the right grip, the straight back-lift and the forward and back movements of the feet, with the head perfectly still.

From then onwards I like to imagine my batting fitting into four distinct compartments. First, rock-like defence, based on the forward defensive stroke and the backward defensive stroke. In these two strokes I have no other thought

in mind but defence of my wicket; I am keeping the ball
out at all costs. Second, the stroke is again mainly defensive.
Just as I am playing the ball I may find, in the last fraction
of a second, that there is time (because I have seen the ball
quite clearly off the pitch) to ease the ball away into a pre-
conceived gap for a quick single. This is the best way to
start any innings. There is not much difference between
absolutely ruthless, stolid defence and the next stage—
precisely the same stroke, in fact, except that at the last
moment I think quickly and with a late wrist action ease
the ball through a gap in the field.

Now, third, let us think in terms of offence. Upon the
same framework I seek to play forward or back. Imagine
that I have seen the ball early in its flight and that it is a
delivery that can be scored off, a delivery which necessitates
my moving into a position from which I can stroke the ball
through a certain gap. There is no thought of the ball
bowling me out or getting me out unless I mishit. I am in
full control; it is for me to dominate the situation. So by
moving early and with no alteration of the basic movement
I can stroke the ball away, relying upon the timing which
comes from a good balance.

Then fourth is a development of this attacking stroke to a
fierce hit, letting myself go with gay abandon. The opportune
moment has arrived, when perhaps I have built up a largish
score, I am on top and the bowler is trying desperately hard
to keep the runs down. All the time I am on the look out
for the good ball, which can bowl the best player out at any
time, but for the most part I shall be seeking to dominate
the situation. I may have thrown the field back so deep
that the timed stroke will not penetrate. This calls for
improvisation, laying aside the set pattern of my technique,
relying more upon the natural, uninhibited method and

hitting the ball in the air—producing a feast of natural strokes, which come easily with a good eye.

There we are, then—four distinct compartments running into each other. Strict defence—defence which can seize on to scoring opportunities, playing them away for singles; then the controlled offence where correct stroke play and good timing can spray holes through the opposition defences with devastating effect, before running riot with gay, abandoned hitting.

First you must learn to build an innings. As you take guard and look round the field you must sum up the situation so as to know at once where a quick single can be taken and where the bad ball must be hit. As the bowler is running up to bowl the first ball, slip the bottom hand right down the handle, keep the back-lift down to a minimum —search for that first ball and keep it out of the stumps as if your life depended upon it. That first ball is vital and breathe a sigh of relief after it has been safely despatched. For a few minutes the accent is on strict defence, although you must always be ready to push the bad ball away to get off the mark. After a few singles confidence is gathering and you will begin to think about those strokes in reserve, but you must not get too excited. Compartment one is beginning to be left behind and it is compartments two and three which monopolize your play from twenty runs to fifty; then from fifty onwards you are in full control and nothing can hold you. You should employ all four methods, blending perfectly to comprise a good innings.

Now let's deal with each stage, one by one.

STAGE 1

Strict Defence Forward

Basic principles comprise back-lift over the off-stump, left shoulder pointed to the bowler and so hiding the right shoulder from view, head square to the bowler, eyes level and very, very still, weight being transferred on to the toes as the ball is delivered; thrust your front leg out, not on a full stretch but on a three-quarter stretch, so that the knee will flex, taking the whole weight of the body. The back leg is left behind, absolutely still, fairly taut, with the toe resting within the crease. Don't thrust the bat right out, way out ahead, because it is merely committing it to the ball to do its worst. Keep the bat under your head, so that your eye can watch the ball on to the bat. Try to keep the chin, the left wrist and the left toe in one perpendicular line on striking and you will find you have as perfectly controlled a defensive forward stroke as you could possibly have. You must aim to put the front foot just inside the line of the ball, with just sufficient room for the bat to come through in a perpendicular straight line. If the ball is on the off-stump or outside remember to move right across so that you push the ball back towards the bowler. It is a great mistake to think just because the ball is wide that you should come to it at an angle and push the ball out towards extra cover, because, quite clearly, you have to angle the bat and the ball could slide off the slant of the bat to slip. The wider the ball is, if you choose to play it, the farther you must move across to play the ball back to the bowler, giving the ball the full square face of the bat. In contrast, if the ball is pitched on the line of the leg stump, or just outside the line of the leg stump, be careful how much you open up the stumps. It is better here in defence, I think, to push the front leg down the line of the leg stump and to let the bat go just in front of the leg, so that you are pushing the ball towards mid-on here. By so doing you are not opening up and thus exposing all three stumps dangerously.

Strict Defence Back

Now, in every back stroke we have the same basic principle: back-lift over the off-stump, weight transferred on to the toes, head absolutely still, square to the bowler, eyes level. You move the back foot to a position twelve inches from the stumps and covering the middle and off-stumps, allowing the bat to swing down the line of the stump. If the ball is pitched to leg stump this can still be a good position, so that the bat is swinging from off-stump down towards mid-on, very slightly across the line. It is better to do this rather than to play back down the line of the leg stump and open up the stumps. If the ball is pitched off-stump you are in a perfect position to play down an absolutely straight line, giving a full square face of the bat to the bowler. If the ball is pitched outside the off-stump try to go farther across with this back foot, so as to cover the off-stump even, or just outside, to ensure the ball going straight back to the bowler rather than to extra cover, and so presenting this angled face to the bat, which might give a catch to slip or to the wicket-keeper.

There it is, then. These two defensive strokes following the same pattern, just a different movement of the feet. In the back stroke, just as in the forward stroke, keep the chin, the left hand and the front foot all in one perpendicular line on striking. This ensures that the eye is in a position to watch the ball right on to the face of the bat.

STAGE 2

This stage is defensive, but looking to score at the slightest opportunity. This stroke comes into being just on the point of striking the ball. After watching the ball off the wicket a last-moment reaction transforms a purely defensive, dead-bat shot into a productive, guided stroke. Off the front foot you may be able to place it into the gap between mid-off and cover if the ball is pitched just outside the off-stump; or if the ball is pitched on the leg stump you can push the ball wide of mid-on. There is no great risk involved, as you are not playing directly across the line. It is just a last-moment manipulation of the bat with the bottom hand, quite safe and very good cricket. As you steer the ball away a quick call 'Yes, run!' will set the two batsmen strolling through for a quick single, which is so good to watch and provides a valuable foundation for any innings.

In the same way, off the back foot we can play these two shots, at the last moment, into the gap between mid-off and cover or just wide of mid-on; but quite as safely, if the ball is off the stumps and one can play it just a little bit later in flight with a perpendicular, straight bat and guide it down through the gully. Or, if the ball is on the leg side, again you can play it a little bit later and guide it down wide of the short legs, and a quick call will find you collecting the vital singles.

It is all very simple and straightforward, provided you have it clearly in mind what to do.

STAGE 3

We saw Stage 2 as a period when the batsman is striving to gain the ascendancy over the bowler, who still holds the whip hand, but as we move into Stage 3 the pressure is easing, the fielders are moving back on the defensive and the batsman is starting to unleash a more full-blooded stroke to pierce the defensive cordon. The batsman becomes much more aggressive as he looks to keep the score moving. During this period he is definitely on top, although the bowler and the fielding captain may retain a certain measure of control in a defensive role.

STAGE 4

The fourth stage is all-out attack, either off the back foot or the front foot. Although you can play the fiercest strokes from orthodox positions, most cricketers start to break the rules at this point. Because the batsman is in such a dominant frame of mind, so full of confidence, there will be no inhibitions to stop him from developing his own methods of taking toll.

Taking Guard

On arrival at the crease the batsman must take guard, and there are three customary positions: middle stump, leg stump and two leg, which is a position half-way between middle stump and leg stump. A batsman must learn to know where his stumps are all the time, for upon his position at any given time depends his judgement of the line of the ball and the selection of a stroke. So, then, the sole purpose of taking guard is to provide the batsman with a navigational aid. It is difficult to lay down reasons why one guard should be better than another, and only experience can teach each individual what is best for him. I always take leg stump, unless I am playing very fast bowling, when I take middle, and even middle and off, so that I do not have to move across the wicket in too much of a hurry.

By taking this guard to Dennis Lillee or John Snow I feel that I am just that fraction of a second better off than if I am taking leg stump. I have to realize that a straight ball at my legs, which I would normally think of pushing round the corner or leg gliding, makes me very vulnerable to an l.b.w. decision. I have to make a rule, then, not to play across the line of the ball unless it appears wide down the leg side. To anything which looks to be bowled at my legs I must play with a very straight bat back to the bowler; anything which looks just wide of the off-stump can be left alone with complete safety. The danger comes with a change of bowling which makes me alter my guard back from middle and off-stump to leg stump. The line of delivery which I was leaving quite safely outside the off-stump will probably knock the off-stump over and this demands extra concentration and self-discipline.

When off-spin bowlers were turning the ball acutely Denis Compton used to have a trick of taking leg stump from the umpire and then moving three or four inches outside it. He maintained that bowlers tended to follow him and by so doing they would be bowling down the leg side and so become less effective, laying themselves open to be hit on to the leg side. He would know that any ball directed towards his leg was a free hit and by opening up in this way he was in a much better position to play his strokes. It also had the advantage of blocking out the leg slips, as he would tend to push the ball away defensively on to the off-side. I have never had the courage to follow his pattern, but I mention his method because it shows how important the question of taking guard was to him in this instance.

I have often been asked why I keep asking for a new guard in the middle of an innings. Often it is simply that the mark that one has made has become obliterated or damaged by other batsmen's studs or a bowler running across. Occasionally I do alter my guard to try to make the bowler try something different, in the hope that this will upset his rhythm, but I try to make a point of seeing that the bowler does not hear me ask. Usually I ask for leg stump and then make my own calculations as to where centre might be. If the fielding side are trying to defend by bowling wide of the off-stump a guard of leg stump makes for such a long stretch to get to the bowling. Here is an obvious instance where the move to middle and off improves your position and might make the bowler bowl straight. You for your part must not be trapped by playing across the line of a dead-straight ball, or else you are playing into his hands; you must be one step ahead of him and in this way turn his trick into runs for yourself.

One thing I must impress upon you: when you take guard and make your mark, usually on the batting crease, cut a straight line with one of your studs, running from near the stump right through to your mark. In this way you will never make a careless mistake with your guard; you will always know which is yours, and, believe me, I have been l.b.w. on several occasions because inadvertently I have slipped into somebody else's guard.

The Forward Drive

The principle is the same for the cover drive, for the off drive, for the straight drive and for the on drive. In each case one is looking for a ball which is over-pitched, ideally a half-volley, but if one is confident enough of the even pace and bounce in the wicket a ball can be hit 'on the up'. English players are very wary of driving anything which is not a clean half-volley because the uncertainty of our wickets has taught them to be cautious. The sight of an overseas player in full flow on English wickets is always an eye-opener to those who have never known anything else but English conditions, and you will always see the old professional nodding his head wistfully, and hear him muttering critically, 'He got away with it, but I don't like it.'

As you make the decision to move into the drive, your left hip turns, showing your back to the bowler, and your left shoulder leans into the stroke. All through the stroke your head must remain square and still as a rock, with the eyes level, never wavering, clearly focussed on the ball. The weight transfers from the back foot on to the front foot, the front foot becomes a very solid platform, but not too stiff; your front knee takes the weight as it bends, but not too much; the front toe points towards the position in which the ball is being directed, that is, in the cover drive the left foot squares up to the bowler and to an on drive your front foot opens out to point to mid-on. After the weight has been transferred the back leg must be balanced on the toe, which is kept clearly behind the popping crease (in case you should miss altogether). In carrying all the weight on the front leg you should be so well balanced that the front foot comes down on to the heel and then up on to the toe. The vital part about this stroke is the position of the ball on the point of impact. If the ball is too far away from the bat it is liable to be lofted; if you leave it too late you may be yorked or you sense the awful feeling of squeezing the ball into the ground to no effect, but to sting the hands. For each stroke there is just one perfect position for complete freedom of movement where you can achieve maximum power in complete safety.

For the on drive the ball should be a little farther away from the bat on striking, because one has got to play the ball very much earlier. For the straight drive you allow the ball to come on just a little bit farther, farther still for the off drive where the ball is almost underneath the head on striking. Then with the square cover drive that Denis Compton used to play so exquisitely the ball should be level with the right shoulder at point of impact.

There is a knack in timing the drive which cannot be explained or taught, but the feel of it comes with experience.

You must try to think of speed of stroke, not strength. After all, the velocity with which the ball is hit depends more upon the speed of the bat flowing through than the strength of the person behind it. Apparently, no one has hit the ball harder than Sir Donald Bradman, a diminutive little figure; the secret lies in being able to hit fast and late —the very term sounding illogical, I know. I can only try to describe it in a glimpse of play when David Allen was bowling slow off-spinners to Rohan Kanhai and I was fielding at first slip. The ball was just beginning to drop when to my horror Kanhai had hardly moved, apart from the normal back-lift. My concentration upon the ball wavered as I wondered whether Kanhai may not have been ready, when in a flash, seemingly too late but in fact at the critical moment, panther-like he sprang into action and, making one perfect, complete stroke, rocketed the ball through the covers.

Naturally I watch a tremendous lot of cricket and wherever and whenever anyone has not executed a stroke properly it can usually be accounted for in one of three reasons. The most common, of course, is that the front foot has not been put near enough to the ball. With a cross bat there is less chance of middling the ball truly. Secondly, the weight is not being transferred properly from the back foot, so at the moment of striking the batsman is leaning back. Thirdly, the stroke is embarked upon too early, so that there has to be a pause, followed by a last-minute stilted jab, devoid of timing and power.

Against a slow bowler a batsman ought to be on the look-out to be moving down the wicket to collect a good-length ball on the full toss or even half-volley. This requires good judgement allied to fast footwork. In this way he can upset a bowler's rhythm and make scoring opportunities from what would otherwise have been defensive prods. This is a positive method, a powerful weapon, which the quick-footed batsman has in reserve at any time and uses all too infrequently. There is less risk in moving down the wicket to the off-spinner than to the ball spinning the other way, for should you be beaten by the spin the ball may be covered by your pads and body.

The Leg Glance

If the ball is not pitched up far enough to drive wide of mid-on but is a good-length delivery, on or just outside the leg stump, there is still a chance to score from it. Play a forward defensive stroke into the ball as though you were pushing the ball to mid-on. Watch the ball particularly carefully off the wicket and keep your eye glued on it until it meets the bat. Just before you feel the ball touch the bat relax the wrists, at the same time turning the blade slightly to leg. You will then find the ball doing all the work, using the middle of the bat to angle itself to long leg. This is a lovely stroke to watch. It looks so difficult and yet there is a simple knack to be picked up after a little practice in a net, the key to it lying in watching the ball very closely. Once learnt it is never forgotten, and you will bless the day that you took the trouble to acquire this most attractive stroke for your armoury. When you have been able to produce it off the front foot then you can think of playing it off the back foot, where it is not quite so easy, because it requires a certain amount of body pivot just as the stroke is being executed, the back foot swivelling. You should meet the ball a few inches in front of the left leg and right underneath your nose, with eye glued to the ball.

Two things to remember: don't attempt to glance a ball off the stumps when to miss the ball altogether brings sudden death l.b.w.; don't attempt to glance a ball which is too wide down the leg side, for you will only give the wicket-keeper the chance of a simple catch.

The Sweep Shot

This is the stroke which causes the downfall of more bats-men than any other stroke I know—purely because people are so careless about the choice of delivery. There is no doubt, also, that you can become 'sweep happy', daring to play it at everything once you catch the bug! There is something contagious about the sweep shot, which is an intensely satisfying stroke to pull off, but I think most batsmen would be better off if they had never heard about it.

However, we have got it, whether we like it or not, and so let me be positive and define its usefulness. It is only contemplated against a slow bowler who pitches the ball on a good length or farther up, just outside leg stump. Never, never, never sweep off the stumps . . . and if you do don't dare to complain about the umpire as you wend your way back to the pavilion! If the ball is a half-volley the front leg is thrown out towards it and the bat is swept across the line horizontally and the wrists are rolled over on impact, so as to keep the ball on the ground. It is easier, quite obviously, to sweep the off-spinner more safely than the leg-spinner, because you are hitting with the spin. The leg-spinner is more likely to fly off the top edge of the bat. Personally, I think this delivery should be hit wide of mid-on, along the ground or in the air, and that the sweep shot is too risky. I much prefer playing the sweep shot to the good-length ball, with the bat not driving horizontally but over in a loop towards the bowler and down on to the ball, helping the ball on with a quite firm and deliberate tap towards long leg. This method avoids any risk of the top-edge catch and is usually going to bring four runs from a part of the field which the captain cannot afford to have manned for this type of bowling. But I reiterate: leave it alone, but if you are addicted discipline yourself very strictly as to what, when and where!

ATTACKING OFF THE BACK FOOT

The Pull Shot

This shot is only called upon when the ball is short-pitched on a good, reliable wicket and for this reason. Overseas players are much more inclined to pull the ball than we are at home. As the term explains, the right foot moves back along the line of the off-stump or outside and the ball is pulled with a cross bat to the on-side. It used to be a much more effective stroke than it is today, when bowlers were more inclined to bowl at the off-stump, with their fielders deployed on that side of the wicket. With more leg-side fielders it is more rewarding to play the back-foot shot with a straight bat through extra cover, and far safer. But there are moments when the situation cries out for the stroke. Move across with the right foot, the right toe pointing almost straight down the pitch towards the bowler, and with your head just inside the line of the ball hit it hard with a cross bat to mid-wicket, at the same time pivoting the body and rolling the wrists over to keep the ball down. It is essential to pivot the body and keep the legs well apart. This was the stroke which Sir Donald Bradman made famous—and I think it is especially useful for a man of short stature, the reason being that it requires very quick body movement on the turn. The bulkier man can flick the identical ball wide of mid-on with more safety with a perpendicular bat being wielded slightly across the line. In my case this is much safer, as I find it difficult to pivot quickly; however, I think this stroke should be left alone against fast bowlers unless you are playing on a good, reliable wicket.

How much should one hit the ball in the air? There is no doubt in my mind that one should practise lofting the ball into selected areas. There is a world of difference between rash slogging and calculated chipping.

M. J. K. Smith is a pastmaster of this art. If you set a leg-side field to him, with an inner cordon of three and two men out in the deep, he will drop the ball over the top of the near cordon, and safely clear of the deep fielders, time and again. This requires confidence and a degree of skill which can only come from concentrated application in practice. I have made this point to urge you to decide on one or two, perhaps three, types of delivery which you would like to despatch in the air to certain very definite areas. Hitting in the air involves risks unless you know what you are doing. I believe it is essential to limit your scope in this way so as to make more certain of success. The trouble with batting is that unless the fielders are generous one can only make one mistake. After you have 'holed out' ignominiously

Barry Richards - controlled attack. Imperious, leisurely, controlled and perfectly balanced, he demonstrates his exquisite square cut: with a roll of the wrists, the weight on the toes and body moving forward, he is in a position to place this ball either side of third man, with all the power in the world.

Frank Hayes - all - out attack, Frank has seen the ball early. There are no inhibitions as he throws his weight onto the front foot, allowing himself plenty of room for the bat to flow through, applying more right hand than usual. Note the position of the head, still and upright, the key to successful batsmanship.

several times, and suffered the remorse which follows such an indignity, you may well be tempted to make a rule that you are going to keep the ball on the ground for the rest of your career.

Such finality is both unwise and unnecessary.

The Hook Shot

The hook shot is similar in principle to the pull shot, but it involves a slightly different line of delivery and the ball is despatched to another part of the field. The pull shot is taken from outside the off-stump and despatched over an arc between mid-on and mid-wicket. The hook shot concerns the ball bowled in direct line with the batsman or down the leg side and, as the term implies, the ball is hooked round into an arc, square leg to fine leg. Clearly if the ball is bowled straight and despatched straight over the square-leg umpire it is difficult to discern whether it was a hook or a pull. But any hook which sends the ball behind square leg must entail a 'helping-on' action, whether along the ground or in the air. The batsman is using the speed of the ball. The best hookers are those who, in moving across, place their heads in direct line with the ball and on striking and pivoting move their heads outside the line.

Again, this is a stroke for the man of short stature and a quick mover. I am only a successful hooker if I plan for it having the stroke in mind when I feel the bowler is after me. In other words I am getting into a position almost before I ought to do so, and I would not advocate this method to anyone. I would go to this trouble occasionally in order to put an end to a short bout of fierce aggression on the part of the bowler. For the most part I am content to duck or dodge the occasional bouncer intended to catch

C

me unawares, hoping for a catch off the gloves. Peace at all costs!

Running the Ball Down

If you see the ball in sufficient time and clearly enough off the wicket you can steer it away either side of the wicket for singles. To a ball short of a length, on or just outside the off-stump, play the ball late, guiding it through the gulley.

Against the medium-fast or fast bowler you can play what appears to be an orthodox defensive stroke, hit from behind the line of the ball, with a straight bat following through to the bowler. By allowing the ball to come on just that extra foot so as to meet it under your head it will deflect quite safely off the middle of the bat along the ground, through the gully. This is what we call running the ball down to third man, using the pace of the ball. It is not a dangerous stroke provided the batsman is in line and well over the top of the ball. The only danger can come when the ball lifts a little more than you expect. Consequently, you must be discerning as to the right time to play this stroke. When you find a captain dispensing with a gully, creating a wide gap down to third man, here is the obvious time, but not if the ball is hard and new or the pitch is showing irregularity of bounce. Often against spin bowlers you will find it difficult to penetrate the cover cordon however well you time your drives, and this is the time to steer the ball down two or three times for a single, wide of slip's outstretched hands. By so doing the fielding captain will be forced to alter the field, which will invariably open up a new gap elsewhere.

The Late Cut

If this same ball is bowled a foot wider of the off-stump this stroke becomes dangerous and the late cut ought to be employed. This calls for a last-minute movement and there is a very distinct knack to achieve the timing. You can decide early to play the late cut, but there is a moment of watching and waiting whilst the ball passes you, and then a quick movement, with the right foot back and across to cover the off-stump. By this time the ball is half-way between the creases and your wrists chop down, with the wrists rolling over the top of the ball. It becomes a dangerous stroke if you move too early or, in waiting for the ball to arrive, you cut underneath the ball, giving the slips and wicket-keeper a chance. The late cut entails what its term implies—a stroke played as late as possible, delicate but precise. The power comes mainly from a quick wrist action, using the speed of the ball. Thus it is unsafe to think about this stroke when the fast bowlers are on with a new ball. Once the ball is softer, and not bouncing quite so fiercely, the safety margin becomes a little wider. The risk of this stroke is governed as much by the type of pitch as the type of bowler—the faster the pitch, the more skill required. This is a stroke which must be reserved for the good player, or the mediocre player right in form and going well; otherwise, it is best left alone.

The Square Cut

To the same-length ball, but wider of the off-stump, the square cut comes into play and can be the most devastating stroke in the game.

It is made with a horizontal blade hitting the ball at the top of its bounce, with the bodyweight leaning forward as the wrists roll over, so as to ensure that the ball is kept down.

On seeing the bowler drop the ball short, the left shoulder should turn into the ball, showing your back to the bowler, and from this position comes the full body pivot, bringing the full weight to the stroke.

Always cut hard with as quick a wrist action as one can develop. It must be a full swing and not a jerk, finishing with a complete follow-through. You can aim to hit the ball either side of cover point and should be able to obtain such control over the direction that no field placing can stop you. It becomes a dangerous stroke when the front shoulder is pulled away too soon, dropping the right shoulder and forcing the bat to hit under the ball. Like the late cut, the back foot is required for a firm platform. Because you play a square cut with a horizontal bat you must expect to have a few air shots. Every now and again a top edge will send the ball flying high over the heads of the slips. The faster you play the stroke, the more likely you are to 'get away' with the mistake, but this is no excuse for an unbalanced slash.

Orthodox Attack

I always feel that the late cut, the square cut, the pull shot and the hook shot are strokes for the quick mover. Alvin Kallicharran and Rohan Kanhai are both of short stature and immensely quick movers. They are both masters of all four strokes.

For my part I rely upon a different range of strokes, aiming to hit the ball in more orthodox fashion, with a straighter bat and leisurely timing, yet selecting my gap just as skilfully.

Barry Richards and Gary Sobers are famous for the way in which they seize on to the short ball (which Sir Donald Bradman hooked and Kanhai square-cuts) and hit it mercilessly through any gap between cover and mid-on. They thump it with a pendulum-like swing of the bat, gracefully, but with all the power in the world. I have set myself to follow their pattern, preferring this type of stroke to the cuts and hooks. Today, with the attack so lop-sided towards the leg side, I have had to master a stroke which flicks the ball off my stumps, wide of mid-on. This is a Barry Richards type of stroke, played with great power. By bringing one's back foot straight down the line of the leg stump one gives the bat room to come down straight before a last-minute roll of the wrists on point of impact can flay the ball to the boundary behind mid-wicket. Peter May was the complete master of this stroke.

Try to play all these strokes off the back foot and you will soon discover which comes to you easily and which do not suit you. Armed with this information, you can then decide on the best method to suit the situation, depending upon the type of bowler, the pace of the wicket, the setting of the field and weighing up the risks involved. This is what I call sensible, calculated batsmanship.

Calling and Running

Whenever I am asked about running between the wickets I shiver with embarrassment at the nightmarish situation Peter Richardson and I found ourselves in at Nottingham in our first Test match together against Australia in 1956. The match was hardly under way when a full house was brought to its feet almost to a man. I drove Miller through the covers for what might have been three or four but for an overnight storm which had drenched the ground. I set off, urging my partner on, in the hopes of several runs. To my horror the ball had slowed up in the wet outfield and when I turned for the second run Davidson had the ball in his hand. I shouted for Peter to wait. He had just set off and promptly applied the brakes, only to find himself skidding in the wet, to end flat on his back seven yards from home. For once in a while something ticked very quickly within me and I streaked off to the other end, knowing that Peter had no chance to recover. Three yards from home the ball passed the stumps, but bouncing so awkwardly that wicket-keeper Langley had to retreat to take it. He had the choice of throwing the ball at my stumps from four yards, with only one stump to aim at, or a quick flick to the other end where Keith Miller could hardly contain himself with excitement, with the scrambling Richardson still a long way to go. Both ends were at his mercy. I was relieved to find Langley judging the other end to be a better proposition and I turned to watch the finish of this charade. Langley threw four feet wide, whilst Miller, clutching at the ball, knocked all three stumps over, and by the time he had gathered it he could do nothing about the situation, for Richardson had flashed past the tapes, leaving eleven Australian fielders aghast and querulous at letting us off the hook. For several minutes the crowd buzzed with excitement and I remember playing the last two balls of the over as if the whole world was whispering in my ear.

We make too little of the value of good running in this country. It involves team-work and partnership, so much depending upon the temperament of the various individuals concerned as to whether they are prepared to co-operate. Each batsman has his own mannerisms and methods of calling which take some getting used to, though I feel it should be a much simpler problem than we tend to make it. The interesting thing about my partnership with Richardson was that we had never met at all, let alone batted together, before that match at Nottingham. This particular mishap was brought about by the wet condition of the ground rather than any mistake between us, and from that moment onwards we were very rarely at variance.

In recent years, Asif Iqbal and I have built up a perfect understanding and it makes batting such fun.

The first rule we made was that we were never going to get angry with each other. It is all too easy to make a call, change one's mind and send your partner scampering home and then to have a glaring session at each other. This breeds lack of trust. We decided at once that nothing was going to be achieved unless we were on the look-out for every opportunity. This meant, inevitably, that there was going to be the odd mistake, requiring a quick call of rescue. It was vital for the man in control at the time to decide one way or the other firmly, and *with all speed*.

In other words, if I struck the ball in front of the wicket and called for a run, as long as I shouted quickly enough Asif would always accept a denial to scamper home in safety, without questioning my decision. At the same time I would not expect him to turn me down. Very occasionally, especially in long partnerships, one has moments when a lapse of concentration finds you slow off the mark, or slow to back-up, and this is a moment for denying one's partner, followed by apology. Of course, if you do not trust your partner—and there may be good reason for your being in this frame of mind—you may have to watch for his calling and deny him frequently, but this is a very unsatisfactory state of affairs.

Let us assume that two of you have got together and are prepared to trust each other implicitly. Already you are two-thirds of the way towards achieving success. The striker should call for everything in front of the wicket and square of the wicket; the non-striker should call for everything

behind the wicket. Restrict your calling to three words—
'Yes', 'No' and 'Wait'. With the ball running in front of
the wicket and behind the wicket, obey your partner's call,
and only question it in dire emergency.

You will find that 75 per cent of the run-outs come from
the indecision caused by the ball that is played square of
the wicket, and I always like to make sure that there is a
very easy run available before setting off. I would much
rather settle for a century partnership, with ten lost singles
through over-caution with the ball running square of the
wicket, than I would suffer the possibility of several close
scrambles which serve only to undermine the confidence
of the partnership. I cannot over-emphasize the dangers
involved in the ball running square of the wicket. Each
batsman tends to gaze at the other, not quite knowing who
is taking charge. From experience I have found that the
striker should always take charge of this situation and that
the non-striker should be looking to obey. Paradoxically,
I believe that it is the non-caller who plays the most important role in a good running partnership. I like to trust
my partner to such an extent where I only watch whether
he has hit the ball in front of the wicket or behind. If the
ball has been played in front or square of the wicket, and
it is clearly his call, I keep my eye fixed on his eye and one
glance will show what we are doing.

David Sheppard and I established a good liaison in
Australia and we helped each other enormously. The only
time I would take my eye off the striker's eye is when he
has quite clearly got the ball down through the gully or
glanced it away to long leg, and then the responsibility is
mine, and mine alone. I would expect his eye to be upon me,
ready to obey. It will not be very long before you establish
such confidence between you that you hardly need to call at all.

It is amazing how many great players have been appalling runners, and, sad to say, selfishness has been the root cause. The worst feature of many great players has been their greediness to hold the strike and their capacity to steal it on the fifth or sixth ball of each over. I am glad to say that throughout my career I have never batted with anyone who has consciously taken away the strike from me against my will. I have always regarded batting as a partnership, and often I have found my partner going so well that I have helped him to keep the strike so as not to lose his productive phase. After a while I may become weary and it is helpful for him to take over the reins. The key to a successful batting partnership is to be found by one of them assuming the dominant role and the other playing a clever second string. This can best be achieved by good, calculated running between the wickets.

John Edrich has brought great skill to this aspect of batsmanship by the way in which he drops the ball down, moving into the quick single with the stroke, and no fielder in the world could do anything to stop it. Bobby Simpson, the Australian captain, was another. When a batsman is being kept quiet by good, defensive bowling, to a well-set field, two alternatives present themselves. One is the calculated risk in lofting the ball over the ring of fielders. Often the stroke may not be quite appropriate to the situation. Secondly, the quick, tapped single. The second method is by far the best proposition, provided there is a close understanding between the two batsmen.

In this situation I always like to discuss the possibilities with my partner—'I am trying to push the ball wide of extra cover', or 'If I can flick it to the on-side, mid-on is very slow and has a bad throw, so I think I can get a run there as well—watch for these two possibilities.'

This brings me to the point that you should always be quick to observe which fieldsmen are quick, which are slow, which have weak arms, who is left-handed, who is right-handed.

As a non-striker I like to stand level with the stumps, and as the bowler delivers the ball I like to walk fairly briskly up the pitch, so that as my partner is playing the ball I am on the move, ready for a sprint if necessary.

Beware of the straight drive back at the stumps, for there can be no more wretched way of getting out than to be run-out like this. Be sure to stand seven or eight feet wide of the stumps to help you run off the pitch, but not to block the view of the fielder behind you. I always accept that he has the right to move you, should he so desire. The non-striker should run wide, allowing the striker to run where he likes, except on the pitch, of course. In this way there is no danger of a collision or any doubt about which lane to run in.

When running several runs you stop short of the crease. Make a habit of dropping your bat over the line rather than risk running it in and out again. I have often had runs taken away from me through trying to slide the bat in, getting it stuck, and in my anxiety to get going again I have taken my eye off those few vital inches and never completed the run. Only run the bat along the ground when you are scrambling for home trying to best the throw, for by doing this one can make maximum use of the ground. It is amazing how few people turn towards the side of the ground on which the ball has been struck when they have completed a run and are in process of embarking upon a second. This is not quite so complicated as it sounds and must facilitate good calling and running.

Be on the look-out for traps. Jack Hobbs was a great

cover point. Often he would allow batsmen to sneak several singles to give them a false sense of security. After a while he would just steal in those extra couple of yards, very discreetly, before the ball was bowled, and at the next opportunity the stumps would be thrown down in a flash with one of the batsmen a long way from home.

I shall never forget an Australian batsman who had assumed that Brian Statham would be rather weary after a long spell of bowling during a Lord's Test match and that they could indulge in an extra run to him with impunity. This happened twice, successfully, but I sensed Brian's rage. It was not very long before the ball was down in his direction again, the second run embarked on, and from beneath the Warner Stand came a lovely return and a run-out, for Brian Statham had as powerful and accurate an arm as anyone in the game.

Occasionally you will drop your bat, scampering for a single. Don't do what I did in my first competitive cricket match, aged eight. I stopped to pick it up and could not believe my eyes that the fielders should be so ungenerous as not to take this into account! I was run out by six yards; I just could not believe that they were serious! However, the lesson went home and it has never happened again.

You must expect to make mistakes and hardly a day will go by without a run-out. You will learn something new each time and each harsh experience will teach you that the basis of good running and calling involves a few simple, straightforward 'dos and don'ts'. Get to terms with them as quickly as you can and you will find yourself master of the subject, rather than bowed down by the fear that every innings will be marred by a run-out.

On the boat to Australia for my first tour I woke up bathed in perspiration several times after a nightmare.

The scene was a Melbourne Test with a huge crowd laughing and cheering because I had run Hutton or Compton out!

Placing the Ball

I have asked all the great players whether they used to make up their minds before a ball was bowled where they were going to hit it. The answers were straightforward—never, never, never make up your mind to hit the ball in a certain place before it is bowled, but be quite certain in your mind of the one or two places you might hit it if a certain type of loose delivery appears. There is all the difference in the world between these two approaches. May I add that every one of those great players would say to me that on certain days when everything was going right for them and the game seemed easy for a change, then they were inclined to pre-select. Such was their confidence and skill on these occasions that their plans would be successful more often than not. But I feel this is a game of guesswork reserved for the truly great. Until you reach those heights you must not decide in advance. But, at the same time, to plan certain gaps in the field is absolutely safe and makes for positive, offensive batsmanship. In fact, the moment we start to think ahead in this way we begin to place the ball according to the field set against us, rather than going through the motions of a stroke merely for the stroke's sake.

Let us imagine a half-volley pitched on a leg stump, which the batsman can play safely anywhere between the bowler and the square-leg umpire, as he chooses. The captain can only afford two fielders in that arc, and to hit the ball directly to the fielder when there are three gaps available is extremely careless. The good captain may strive to block the straighter strokes by placing a straight mid-on and a wide mid-on. He is virtually saying to the batsman, 'You won't pierce that part of the field and if you want to hit the ball for four you must hit it square and so play across the line.' In certain circumstances this may be too great a degree of risk. Here the batsman has to weigh up his own form, the state of the pitch and the skill of the bowler, as to whether the risk is justified.

It may be that he will have to compromise by cutting out the drive to the boundary and resort to pushing the ball carefully—but quite deliberately—into the gap for a single or possibly two runs. Here is just one illustration. There is endless scope and variety for the batsman in this art of placing the ball and there is nothing more demoralizing to a fielding captain and his toiling bowlers than the batsman who takes the initiative and refuses to be pegged down by the bowler's tactics.

Left-handers

I have two young sons, one of them a right-hander and the younger one stands naturally as a left-hander. When anyone has tried to turn the younger one round to stand right-handed he has looked most uncomfortable and clearly does not enjoy it. Should one leave him to play left-handed? At what point should one try to force him to be different? Anyway, why not encourage him to be a left-hander?

Sobers and Harvey have been the best left-handed batsmen I have seen, and yet had Bert Sutcliffe, the New Zealander, had more opportunity of top-class cricket he could have been in their class. John Edrich is the best English left-hander, with tremendous powers of concentration, and he is a prodigious run scorer. I admired Graeme Pollock who, like the great Frank Woolley, made the game look so easy. He had every-thing. Quick footwork, perfect balance, beautiful timing, a very complete range of strokes, all these made him an ideal model for any youngster—left-handed or right-handed.

Neil Harvey and now Younis Ahmed have boasted something of the same facility, but they developed various unorthodox strokes of their own which I would never wish anyone to copy. They have succeeded because they have had a flair, that spark which is inborn and can never be produced or taught.

Neil Harvey found it easier to grip the bottom of the handle with his left hand and from an early age looked more proficient that way round: yet he plays tennis, billiards, squash, throws from the outfield or writes letters, all with his right hand. He was lucky to find a coach early on who was himself a left-handed batsman. This gave him extra encouragement. His coach implanted a feeling of 'one-up-manship' from being a left-hander, in that bowlers never relished the prospect of bowling to a left-hander, nor did they find it easy to change their line of attack when he came to the crease. In this respect I am sure that the left-hander has a significant advantage; in fact, by and large, he enjoys many more advantages than he has hardships.

His only serious hardship involves the rough which is caused by the footmarks of the bowler's run-through. In a one-day match a left-hander who has to bat towards the end of the day is bound to find footmarks on the pitch, especially on English grounds where the wickets are soft. Here an accurate spinner will cause havoc. In three-day cricket a left-hander will always find it harder going in the second innings.

In the hard school of Test cricket you will find skilful bowlers coming round the wicket at the left-hander, so as to pitch the ball into the rough. By using the angle of coming round the wicket it poses a real problem to the left-hander. This, one feels, borders on to the 'fair and unfair' play clause, and, as a captain, I have never felt entirely happy about allowing bowlers to do it. For this reason the new 'no-ball' experiment which brings the bowler's front foot back has contributed a valuable by-product in that it brings the bowler's footmarks back that vital two feet nearer the batsman, sufficient to make the rough a half-volley length. Thus that dangerous delivery now becomes less of a threat.

But it is the change of direction required which upsets a bowler's rhythm most of all, and thereby saps his confidence. Time and time again I have seen a bowler who was going from strength to strength have his confidence shattered by the advent of a left-hander. Left-handers are nearly always particularly strong on the leg side, and the bowler, in pushing the ball across to his off-stump, has to alter the swing of his body action. This is the cause of the bowler's rhythm being upset. Leg-spinners are never the same bowlers against left-handers, as they cannot get as much spin from the pitch when they have to push the ball wide of the off-stump.

The orthodox slow left-hand bowler presents the most dangerous proposition when the wicket is turning, because to miss the ball altogether exposes the risk of l.b.w. One always feels that the off-spinner should be the most dangerous, and often he is, but so often, like the leg-spinner to the right-hander, he will beat everything with no reward for his great skill.

The most dangerous ball from the right-hand fast bowler is the late away swinger to a right-handed batsman. Now this same ball to a left-handed batsman, which will start on a line of his off-stump and appear to be going across the batsman towards first slip, will suddenly duck in late to hit the stumps or find the batsman hopelessly in front l.b.w.

Herein lies a great difficulty to the left-handed batsman. Not many away-swing bowlers can start the swing once the ball is directed wide of the off-stump. Once they start bowling at a left-hander's off-stump the ball tends to keep going on in that direction.

I have seen Freddie Trueman succeed in the first two or three overs with the new ball, but then, as the shine decreases, so did he become less of a threat to the left-handed batsman. Consequently, the best bowler to left-handers in my experience, was Leslie Jackson of Derbyshire and England. With a perfect position of the body at the moment of delivery, where his left foot landed in front of the stumps, he was able to propel the ball along a line from middle stump to middle stump. He was, predominantly, a seam bowler, and with this Jackson was able to secure more l.b.w. decisions against left-handers than any other bowler I know. It was all just a simple matter of straightening up the angle.

Geoff Arnold of Surrey has worried Lloyd and Sobers, and Massie of Australia has produced a similar sort of threat.

In the last twenty years we have seen as great a left-hand cricketer as the game has known and one who could rank with Frank Woolley. As an all-round cricketer Garfield Sobers must be the greatest who has ever walked on to a cricket field. As a swing bowler with the new ball he is fully Test class; he is a more than useful chinaman and googly bowler; he is a useful, orthodox left-arm spinner; he is a very great close catcher, an outstanding deep fielder with a powerful arm. But as a batsman alone he is a brilliant stroke-maker. No one can hit the ball harder, no one has such a natural skill and, with all that, he is very correct in defence.

I am sure that his image and example will inspire a completely new host of young left-hand batsmen all round the world, and the next generation of left-handed batsmen will look more natural than many of their predecessors.

D

2

BOWLING

IN THE very early days of cricket the batting belonged to the rich landowner and his guests, while the bowling was left to the hirelings. Even when the game had developed to the extent where a County Championship was contested it was only the amateur who was given the opportunity of becoming the best batsman and the professionals were still called upon to bear the brunt of the bowling. This suggests, straight away, that batting is an easier life and bowling is hard work. Bowling is a less glamorous art than batting, unless you are an outstanding fast bowler. The cricketing public pay more attention to the performances of the batsmen than to bowlers. The bowler may produce a fine spell of consistent defensive bowling on a perfect wicket, but it will be the batsman's century which will receive the spontaneous applause from the onlookers. The average spectator tends to think that everything revolves round the batsman and the bowler is merely there as a prop.

Over recent years, however, the art of bowling has come to be more widely understood, with the result that a more sensible evaluation of the bowler's merit has emerged. Today, then, it is no longer a labour of love, nor a hobby, for the strong-arm brigade.

Basic Skills

It is often said that top-class bowlers are born and not made —this may well be true. But whereas good batsmanship is dependent upon a sharp eye, anyone could become a reasonably good bowler. Certain basic skills can be taught if the pupil has the will to learn and to go on learning.

Certainly if I had my time again I would prefer to be a bowler than a batsman. Unlike his team-mates, the bowler is always in the game; he can make mistakes and still make up for them—a luxury not afforded to batsmen. The many hours spent in the field can be very tedious for the batsman who does not bowl, but the bowler is always planning and scheming, preparing for the moment to strike; in this way most of the leading bowlers I have known have worked just as hard when they have been taking their rest. Concentrating on trying to detect batsmen's weaknesses, they can be preparing tactics for their next spell of bowling.

It is a good idea, too, for the bowler to listen to all the comments of his fellow fielders, especially the wicket-keeper and the slips, who are so close to things. After all, the bowler aims to dismiss the batsmen as cheaply as possible and he must not let any opportunity slip. Above all, he must develop an attacking frame of mind. There are going to be occasions when it will be necessary to bowl defensively, merely to save runs, but generally speaking he should be attacking the stumps all the time. This is of paramount importance when a new batsman arrives at the crease. Every batsman is on tenterhooks for the first few deliveries and seeks to settle down as quickly as possible, and here is the bowler's chance to break through quickly. He must make it as difficult as possible for the batsman by forcing him to play every ball.

This must be supported by a well-set field in attacking positions. The presence of close fieldsmen tends to upset the batsman's concentration early on and makes him wary of playing full, natural strokes for fear of making a stupid mistake.

It is an old maxim 'A bowler only bowls as well as a batsman allows him to'. There is, of course, a lot of truth in this, but if the bowlers are experienced enough I contend that one could just as well say that a batsman will bat only as freely as a bowler allows him to. The focus is, and always has been, upon the batsman and the bowler is very rarely given credit for restricting the batsmen's scoring opportunities.

Although the bowler should adopt an attacking frame of mind, seeking to dismiss each batsman as soon as possible, there are times, quite obviously, when he has to adopt a varied method of attack. Some batsmen do not like playing through two or three consecutive overs without scoring; they grow impatient to get 'off the mark'. If then an accurate spell of bowling, supported by a well-placed field, induces a rash stroke that earns a wicket this is good, sensible bowling and full marks to the bowler.

How often have you heard the comment about some batsman, 'He was playing so sensibly, why did he have to play a shot like that!' It was overlooked that the bowler and fielders had built up the pressure by restricting scoring chances, so that he had become impatient.

Bowlers work well in pairs. There is nothing more exasperating to the skilful bowler than to find runs being frittered away carelessly at the other end. But if both bowlers are bowling accurately the batsman's task becomes increasingly difficult and the bowlers find themselves in full control. Co-operation between bowlers in this way can mean a great deal to the captain, and one can quote no end of great combinations of bowlers over the years who have helped each other more than the casual spectator would notice. I think Brian Statham helped more colleagues content with his lot in life. Invariably he had to accept ruthless and determined efficiency he did everything

O'Reilly and Grimmett were a great Australian spin-bowling combination and Ramadhin and Valentine were triumphant for the West Indies. Laker and Lock were a prodigious partnership in English cricket, and who will forget the occasion at Manchester when they bowled together hour after hour, with Laker collecting nineteen slices of the cake out of twenty, whilst poor Tony Lock had to be content with one.

Too much importance is placed upon individual efforts with regard to bowling, and averages are an infernal nuisance. All captains would agree that it is the balance of their attack which is all-important, not one outstanding individual. At the same time each bowler must make his own contribution, and this entails bringing all his intelligence to bear in bowling to a plan. A bowler matures and graduates the moment he ceases to be content with merely going through the motions and starts to think what he is trying to achieve. But this is no use at all without the ability to pitch the ball where he chooses. Without such control he cannot start to bowl to a plan, so this must be the first aim of every young bowler.

Most of the great bowlers have a very mean streak when they have the ball in their hands. They are loth to give anything away unless it is part of a plan to get the batsman out. There are occasions when a fast bowler will drop a few bouncers to a good hooker, knowing that it could give away several boundaries, but, in the process, sets the trap to induce a mishit. It really depends upon the state of the game. On a bad wicket, where runs are at a premium, the captain cannot afford such tactics. Under these conditions, of course, runs saved are worth their weight in gold and the bowler cannot try to buy his wicket with so few runs to play with.

For the most part the bowler must aim to bowl straight to a good length, erring to the off-side rather than to the leg side, aiming for a consistency which will enable the captain to set his field more easily. He must not be discouraged if the stumps are not being knocked over as often as he would like, because there are nine other fielders and a wicket-keeper to help him dismiss the batsmen. It is too easy to forget this when formulating the plan. The wicket-keeper ought to be the greatest ally to a bowler because he has the closest view of all. I used to field first slip when Godfrey Evans kept wicket and it was fascinating to hear him discussing various schemes with the bowlers throughout the match. They may not always have proved to be successful, but the value lay in the feeling of a team effort and the spirit engendered.

First of all, then, the young bowler must aim to achieve a sufficient measure of control to enable him to bowl to a plan.

Getting the Batsman Out

Let us review what a bowler is allowed to do under the rules of the game.

Strangely enough, with all the publicity concerning throwers, draggers and changing of the no-ball rule, the bowler is not quite as restricted as one might think. He can bowl right arm or left arm, he can bowl over the wicket or round the wicket, he can bowl within four feet of either side of the stumps—that is, within the return of the creases, which, as you all know, are marked out quite clearly. He must place his front foot behind the popping crease and at the point of delivery his arm must be straight, not bent at the elbow.

All cricket lovers became sick to death with the over-publicized problems of throwing and dragging. Under the new rules dragging has slowly died a natural death, because the back foot is no longer the yardstick. The umpire is only concerned to see that the front foot is behind at the popping crease.

Throwing will always be a problem. The out-and-out 'chucker', whose action is suspect with every ball, presents a problem which is plain for all to see, if not to handle. Much more difficult is the bowler who, when striving for that little extra in an emergency, calls upon a different action, a knack which he has developed, often unwittingly, and which under the laws of cricket is quite illegal. The umpires' task in checking this malaise is an unenviable one and so onerous that M.C.C., in their wisdom, have appealed to cricket authorities the world over to take it upon themselves to stamp it out and thus relieve the umpires.

Mention of fast bowlers brings to mind the comparatively recent addition to the laws of the game concerning 'fair and unfair play'. Persistent and systematic bowling of fast, short-pitched balls at the batsman standing clear of his wicket is unfair, and if in the opinion of the umpire at the bowler's end this is taking place he must call things to order. It was the 'body-line' series in 1932–3 which started off the controversy which made it necessary for the law to be introduced. The tactics of Larwood and Voce were to bowl on the line of the batsman's body with the ball consistently kicking high into the ribs, inducing catches to a line of leg fielders. This dangerous and hostile attack was contrary to the true spirit of cricket. Under today's rule, then, there is nothing to stop a fast bowler from delivering the occasional short ball or bouncer which without the packed leg-side field is a vastly different proposition, for it is not a persistent form of attack. It is difficult to justify the use of the bouncer, which, after all, is intended as an intimidatory weapon, but the longer I play, the more I am convinced that as long as it is properly controlled by the umpires and captains the bowler must be allowed this weapon.

There are one or two other aspects about the condition of the ball which ought to be emphasized. The bowler is not allowed to use anything to help him grip the ball, although there is nothing to prevent a new-ball bowler rubbing the ball on his shirt or trousers in an effort to keep some shine or polish on the cover. 'Shine' is much sought after by the faster bowlers to assist their swing and at the moment there is nothing within the laws to prevent this. With the predominance of seam bowling marring the cricket scene today, it may well be that we shall see a move from the International Conference to restrict polishing to the first twenty-five overs of the new ball.

For the spin bowler, he cannot get rid of the shine quick enough, for the rougher the surface, the better the grip. Drastic measures are often necessary when the pitch is helping the spin bowler and the captain is not wishing to waste precious time by waiting for the quicker bowlers to take the shine from the ball. Under the present laws there

Dennis Lillee leaping high. Dennis Lillee has reached the end
of his run - up and leaps high in the air. Note that his head is in
the perfect position, and that his eyes are still focussed on the
batsman from behind the left arm. The right foot is preparing
to make the platform from which he can unleash a thunderbolt -
the firmer the platform, the better his control.

Bedi and Gibbs - a left and a right. Two masters of weaving long spells of spin and flight demonstrate the value of poise and balance in the delivery stride.

Derek Underwood never gives a batsman a moment's peace.
He is a master of length and line and if the wicket helps him
he can bowl a side out in two hours.

is nothing to stop the spin bowler rubbing the ball on the ground to roughen the surface. In a Test match, not so long ago, one of the captains complained to his opposite number on two counts. First, he complained that certain of the faster bowlers were inclined to run their fingers through well-greased hair which, in its turn, would assist the polishing process. Second, it was noticeable that when a certain bowler was bowling the stitches of the seam had been raised out of all proportion to the general wear and tear of the ball. By lifting the seam with a strong fingernail it was possible for the spinning finger to apply some purchase on the ball. Both these crimes are committed daily and are quite illegal.

I was lucky enough to play in the same county side as that great English spin bowler Douglas Wright, who was inclined to suffer from very dry hands. Partly because of this, and partly because it became a nervous habit, he would lick his fingers just prior to commencing his long, kangaroo run to the wicket. No one ever thought to check this until an overseas umpire regarded it as sharp practice. After consultation with the two captains and the umpires Douglas Wright was completely exonerated, and there was certainly nothing in the laws against it. Sticking plaster causes problems and cannot be used on the bowling hand without the permission of the opposition captain.

One of the most objectionable forms of unfair play comes from a bowler running on to the pitch after he has delivered the ball and creating rough on a good length quite deliberately. I have seen this happen in all grades of cricket and nothing is more undermining to the friendly spirit which may exist between two sides. I have seen a left-arm bowler change from bowling round to over the wicket merely to assist his colleague, an off-spinner, who would come on at the other end to pitch into his footmarks. This is indefensible and there is no condemnation worthy of the captain who condones it.

If an injury forces a bowler off the field for treatment the captain cannot call on that bowler again during that session. In the Kent and Gloucestershire match at Canterbury in 1961 the game was stopped and a knotty point posed to the umpires. Kent were chasing 222 runs for victory and after Dixon and Leary had contributed 91 runs in an hour, only 56 more were needed for victory with five wickets in hand. Then came a surprise. Sam Cook, the veteran and highly skilful Gloucestershire slow left-arm bowler, had not fielded all day, due to a sore finger. At the start of the Kent innings I, as Kent captain, had given the Gloucestershire captain permission for a twelfth man to take the field because I was told that Sam Cook was in an unfit condition to take any further part in the match. Suddenly, at a moment when Kent seemed set for victory and the various Gloucestershire bowling permutations had been exhausted, Tom Pugh, the Gloucestershire captain, waved for Sam Cook to come on to the field. The following over he was thrown the ball and invited to bowl. With that, the umpires consorted and I was called on to the field to join the discussion. To my astonishment there was nothing in the laws to prevent him from bowling. He bowled five overs, taking two quick wickets for 7 runs, the scales were tilted and Kent had lost the match by 24 runs. Here, it seemed, the laws had left a loophole yet again, and it is up to the captains and players to see fair play.

Basic Principles
How can we acquire mastery of length and direction? Such control is not going to come easily, and demands continuous

concentrated practice. But first of all one has to have the picture clear.

A bowler with a free, easy run-up and action is more likely to achieve a greater degree of accuracy than the man with an uneven, erratic delivery. Do not think for one moment that each bowler should be moulded into a set pattern. We are all built differently and, accordingly, each one will develop his own natural method. Every boy can turn his arm over and bowl some kind of delivery, but in the case of those to whom it does not come easily it will soon be apparent that the necessary co-ordination of mind and muscle is lacking. But even to these boys good coaching and constant practice can bring about a definite improvement if they are keen enough and determined to learn.

The most valuable thing for youngsters is that they should see well-known bowlers in action. All lads are born imitators and after watching a particular bowler they will try to emulate him as much as they can. This will produce a combination of their own natural ability, allied to certain aspects which they have picked up from their mentor. Obviously, one hopes that the bowler they have chosen as a model is reasonably orthodox.

There is no set, perfect orthodox action and the best advice one can give to a youngster is to bowl in the way which suits him, although he is wise to have regard for certain basic requirements.

The key to a good action is a good run-up to the wicket. First a bowler must decide how many paces he requires according to the style of his bowling, his strength and weight. Here one can never lay down hard-and-fast rules, but, generally speaking, bowlers tend to take too long a run. Decide on the run you think, then experiment by taking two paces off it and see if it hinders you in any way at all. In this way you will have made quite certain for yourself.

Peter Loader used to have a very long run, one felt, and, moreover, he did not appear to make maximum use of it. When he first travelled overseas he was strongly advised to cut it down as a sensible move to combat the heat. He could never settle to it and explained later that he needed the extra few paces to acquire that important rhythm which only he could feel and of which nobody else could be conscious.

The aim of the run-up is to achieve the maximum performance with the minimum effort. The bowler must decide on a run-up which will enable him to be fully poised and balanced at the moment of delivery, without straining. He must avoid all tenseness and be as relaxed as possible, because it is at the moment of delivery that the real effort comes. Once you have decided on the length of run-up then you must stick to it, both in practice and in match play, so that one drops into the same footmarks day after day after day, and could go through the motions in one's sleep. The perfection of a natural run-up is something that all bowlers should establish as quickly as possible.

The young bowler should strive for a nice easy approach to the wicket, avoiding unnecessary hops and flourishes. In order to gain full impetus and to get the feet into the right position just prior to delivery he will have to spring the last pace before delivering the ball. The jump should not necessarily be a high one, although a lot of great bowlers use a big leap, so as to make a more solid base from which to deliver. Often it is a help to approach the wicket at a slight angle in order to get the left shoulder leading as you move into the delivery stride.

To sum up: As few paces as you can to get maximum

mpetus; a smooth, easy approach to the wicket, coming from an angle; a spring into the delivery stride—all this makes for a good run-up.

From run-up we must then dwell upon action, and, of course, a good action is essential—more essential to the quicker bowlers than to the slower ones. While there are often many successful slow bowlers with peculiar actions, there are not many successful pace bowlers who have looked cumbersome. A simple study of dynamics would show one that the easier and more fluent the action, the more accurate the bowler will be. Following an easy approach to the wicket, we must seek for an easy and natural action. It is extremely difficult to change one's basic action once you have become set in a certain way, but it is possible to smooth out the rough edges.

A golfer is most likely to be successful if he has been clever enough to reach the correct position at the top of the back swing. Most of his difficulties are then over. So with the bowler, and the beginning of a good action comes from the position of the left shoulder. Just before the moment of actual delivery the left shoulder should be pointing very slightly in the direction of fine leg; the left arm must be raised aloft and should automatically point in the same direction as the shoulder. This enables the bowler to keep his eye fixed on the batsman, behind the left arm and over the left shoulder. The bowler should not look at the batsman on the right-hand side of his left arm. Although the left hand need not be stiff, it must be well above the head or otherwise the whole power and rhythm in the action will be lost. By insisting upon the strict position of the left shoulder we avoid the open-chested action which has baulked the progress of so many aspiring bowlers. They remain 'arm-bowlers' who can never use a full body swing at the point of delivery. The young bowler should be made to get this basic position right, and although at first the results may be disappointing because he tends to lose the control which he might have had—he must persevere. He will find it difficult to let the ball go at the right moment, many of his deliveries straying wide to leg, because the twisting of the shoulders and hips makes an accurate release of the ball quite a delicate operation. He will wake up the next morning so stiff that he will never want to bowl again! If the young protégé feels all these problems he knows that he is on the right track to the top. Practice and more practice is then the order of the day.

It is good advice to raise the bowling arm as high as possible, brushing the ear maybe, for this projects the ball down at a steeper angle, encouraging lift, and any deviation through the air or off the wicket will be sharper and more effective. The release of the ball is something which comes quickly and spontaneously, and to obtain the best result the ball must leave the hand just after the left foot hits the ground. It is imperative to ensure that the left foot hits the ground hard and the leg is really braced. After all, from the moment you jump into the delivery stride, first the weight is taken on to the back of the foot, then for a moment the catapult prepares itself for action and then all the weight must be transferred on to the solid base of the front foot. Too many bowlers bend the front leg when delivering the ball and ruin their whole action. As the weight goes on to the front leg the body is thrown into the delivery, before surging ahead again by the front foot pivoting. The right foot comes down again, braced but ready to spring away from the pitch.

This may sound very complicated, but is, in fact, a fairly natural movement. You must aim to achieve a complete half-turn of the hips and shoulders to eliminate as much check or jerkiness in the action or follow-through as you can. Let the follow-through come on until the impetus of the run gradually fades away. Beware of checking too soon after delivery, because the jar and strain placed on the legs and body make one very prone to injury just at this moment.

Control

The machine should be geared for action by now. The next step is to see how accurate it is. Every bowler seeks for the perfect combination of length and direction.

Derek Underwood, as a young eighteen-year-old Kent left-arm bowler, captured 100 wickets in his first full season —no mean achievement. If you watched him in a net for ten minutes you would regard him as just another bowler, for he has no outstanding tricks, but he observes the basic principles of bowling, which bring success in every class of cricket. Ruthlessly and consistently, he bowls day after day, to a perfect length and a very good line. Perhaps his direction is better than his control of length, and this is a good thing. In his case he is a glutton for work; each over he bowls he seems to regard as practice for the next; if he bowls six days in a week he wants to bowl on the seventh, and if the pattern of our English climate did not ordain winter to follow summer Underwood would be bowling from September to April, with a few hours off for food and sleep. There is no easy way to master control and his example of concentration and determination is an object lesson to any aspiring youngster.

Alec Bedser used to place a piece of newspaper on a good-length spot and with half a dozen balls and a net he would toil hour after hour, day after day, striving to improve his consistency.

I think it is important to reduce the length of the pitch for youngsters. There is nothing worse than seeing the young twelve-year-old straining on a twenty-two-yard net wicket. At my junior school we were encouraged to play on an eighteen-yard pitch until we were eleven—then on a twenty-yard pitch until we were thirteen. I do not believe this is shelving the issue because as one grows in strength and stature so it will come quite easy to apply basic techniques to the extra three or four yards.

So, then, we have considered the question of the bowler's run-up, the mechanics of the action and the question of gaining control of length and direction. Let us now consider the various methods which can be used in the middle.

Fast Bowling

Fast bowlers require physique and stamina, not necessarily brute strength. The big, heavy man who makes a good second-row forward is usually too slow in his movements. Three of the greatest fast bowlers, Harold Larwood, Freddie Trueman and Ray Lindwall, have been shortish, stocky men, all of them very good athletes, extremely fast runners, supple, yet with powerful shoulders and hips. Their smooth but fast approach to the wicket has helped to build an image of hostility, for, after all, nothing is more frightening than the fast bowler who races up to the wicket breathing fire and slaughter. At the same time the most awkward fast bowlers to deal with in my experience have been the tall ones, like Keith Miller, Frank Tyson and Gordon Rorke, all of whom had the ability to hit the pitch with a resounding thump and make the ball lift sharply. The shorter man bowls a bouncer which skids on you in a disconcerting way, but he usually has to drop it that much shorter, giving the batsman more time to ease himself out of the line.

Fast bowling makes such demands upon the physical resources of a bowler that he has to keep himself in peak condition, taking special care of his legs and back muscles. There is a tremendous strain on his groin muscles as he pivots, and studs can be a menace when they hold in hard ground. Most of the injuries occur either very early on in the day, before a bowler has properly warmed to his work, or when he begins to tire. Fast bowlers require nursing in shortish spells and they are seen at their best in three-to-four-over bursts. They react rather like racehorses, who can be ruined by overwork.

There seem to be two distinct methods for the fast bowler. Either he can run up as fast as he can, in order to reach maximum speed, whether it be bouncer, yorker or good-length ball. He cannot expect complete accuracy, but he is trusting to his hostility to bring results. Or, by way of variation, he can slow down to some extent, relying on basic skills, swinging the ball in the air or hoping for the seam to do some work off the pitch.

Medium-paced Bowling

The medium-paced bowler is the most valuable contributor to any team. At best these bowlers provide the perfect foil to a genuinely fast bowler at the other end. The fast bowler can then be given the wind, slope or any other conditions to favour him. With his powerful physique and economical run-up the medium-paced bowler can be given the 'donkey' work, and, because he is not exerting himself so violently as the fast bowler, he should have extra staying power. Maurice Tate and Alec Bedser, both with stout hearts and powerful frames, are perhaps the two best medium-paced bowlers the game has ever known. In contrast to fast bowlers, medium-paced bowlers must be accurate to be

E

successful. They must have a certain control of swing in both directions. They will probably be able to seam the ball effectively when the conditions are helpful; also they should develop a strong enough middle finger to produce a dangerous cutter.

Slow Bowling

Fast bowlers have to be youngsters and will reach their prime in their early twenties. The art of slow bowling, on the other hand, is very seldom learned under thirty. Fast bowling requires the fire of youth, whereas the basic skills in slow bowling take many years to develop. It is interesting to note that Frank Tyson hit the headlines aged twenty-four and had disappeared from the scene by the time he had reached thirty. Yet that great Kent leg-spinner 'Tich' Freeman never bowled a ball in first-class cricket until he was twenty-eight and was still bowling in his forties. Jack Iverson, the freak finger-spinner from Victoria, stepped out of a bank straight into the Australian side at the age of thirty-five, having had very little previous experience.

The Off-spinner

Let us study the various types.

The advantage of the off-spinner is that he can bowl more accurately than any other type of bowler. It is the most natural type of delivery, utilizing the natural swing of the arm and position of the body. Where the wickets are responsive to spin, varying in character from day to day, as in this country, the off-spinner is bound to be successful, economical and penetrative. English conditions are ideal for the off-spinner provided that the wickets are not fully covered, and, consequently, most of the counties can boast one. Prior to the change of the l.b.w. law in 1935, when the ball pitching outside the off-stump yet turning into the stumps could not earn an l.b.w. decision, the off-spinner was not so dominant. From the moment the rule was changed his future was assured and his influence has made itself felt more and more.

The off-spin is imparted by the index finger, which in delivering the ball is turned outwards and downwards by a co-ordinated turn of the fingers and wrist. The ball is spun from left to right and the action of the hand is identical to that used in turning a door-knob to the right. The second finger assists the first finger in producing spin but it does not actively contribute quite so much, whilst the third and fourth fingers really become a shelf for the ball to sit on. The thumb acts as a balancing agent, and this, possibly, will vary according to the size and flexibility of the bowler's hand. The swing of the shoulder and body plays a big part and it is important in the delivery stride that the left foot is placed in a line between wicket and wicket, so as to assist the swivel of the body. 'Toey' Tayfield, the great South African off-spinner, used to make a little hole with his left foot about twelve inches in front of the middle stump, with the result that his arm would propel the ball along a line which came from almost round the wicket. This was the reason behind him having so many victims caught at slip, in that a perfectly straight ball of his would be veering slightly across the batsman towards the slips.

Nearly everyone who can bowl at all will produce some sort of off-spinner, as it comes quite naturally, but the good off-spinner must have long, powerful and flexible fingers. Even these attributes will not guarantee that the off-spinner will turn the ball on good, hard, fast wickets to be found overseas. Consequently, the off-spinner does not abound so much in Australia or West Indies, and when he does he either becomes the quicker version who bowls off-cutters, like John Goddard or Denis Atkinson from Barbados—or the slower variety who flight the ball skilfully, like Lance Gibbs. When Jim Laker went to Australia in 1958–9 there were several Australian batsmen out to avenge his great triumph at Manchester in 1956, when the conditions were all in his favour. 'Wait until we get him on our ground,' they murmured amongst themselves, but to his eternal credit he bowled magnificently throughout in conditions where the ball hardly spun at all. Such was his skill and control that he was able to leave the country unscathed. Moreover, he and Tayfield are the only two off-spinners who have ever been consistently successful in all conditions.

The off-spinner must aim to bowl over the wicket most of the time. He should only go round the wicket for variation. On really helpful wickets, where the ball is turning square, he ought to go round the wicket so as to have a better chance of obtaining an l.b.w. decision.

One of the biggest fallacies of modern cricket is that nearly all off-spinners like to bowl round the wicket to left-handers and yet most left-handed batsmen will tell you that they prefer to have the off-spinner bowling round the wicket rather than over the wicket. I would urge all off-spinners to attack the left-hander first from over the wicket. Again, only go round if the ball is turning sharply on a bad wicket.

There are two basic variations which the off-spinner can employ and they are dependent upon the height of the arm. With the arm at its most perpendicular the maximum spin can be imparted. As the arm becomes lower and the line of the trajectory slightly angled, there is a tendency to under-spin, where the ball will start to float away towards the slips, and, on pitching, will skid on rather than hold back. Many a batsman will play and miss at this type of delivery as he makes allowances for spin which does not materialize.

The main ways an off-spinner traps his victim are l.b.w., caught at slip, leg slip or by the wicket-keeper or bowled. The best line for him to bowl is at or just outside the off-stump, so that when the ball turns a fraction it could hit the off-stump. The ball that keeps going straight on gives the wicket-keeper or first slip a chance off the outside edge and for this reason first slip becomes the most valuable fielder to the off-spinner. The only time he may be dispensed with is when the ball is gripping consistently on a bad wicket, with the bowler operating round the wicket. The bowler should tempt the batsman to play defensively forward all the time, hoping for him to leave the fatal gap between bat and pads. Then, by variation, a quicker, lower, trajectory delivery, well pitched up, will often trap the batsman l.b.w. in front of his stumps. The leg slips and short legs come into play as soon as the ball begins to turn sharply.

Mention must be made of Tayfield's plan of bowling defensively on good wickets overseas, where he would station two deep silly mid-ons, standing close to each other eight yards from the batsman. He would seek to pitch the ball up, just short of half-volley, consistently, asking the batsman to drive. This brought these two outstanding fielders some sensational goalkeeper-like catches, and in the process defensive bowling was turned into a trap for attacking batsmen.

Since the change in the l.b.w. law in 1935, the off-spinners have come into their own. Although they will always be a force to be reckoned with on variable wickets, the success of Tayfield and Laker has proved that there is a place for them on the best type of wicket provided that they are accurate enough and have sufficient control of their variation.

The Wrist-spinner

In this category comes the leg-spinner, the top-spinner, the chinaman and the googly. The chinaman, of course, is bowled by the slow left-hander from the wrist, the ball pitching on the right-hander's off-stump and breaking in towards the leg. The slow left-hander's googly comes out of the back of the hand and pitches on the right-hander's leg stump and breaks away to the off. The slow right-hand bowler bowls a leg-spinner and top-spinner, which is helped by a turn of the wrist, and his googly comes from the back of the hand, pitched on the right-hander's off-stump and breaking into the leg. The spinning agent in each case is the third finger; the first two fingers and the thumb are maintained in a comfortable balancing position, but there is a wide gap between the second and third fingers. As a leg break is about to be delivered the palm of the hand is practically facing the batsman, and, as the ball is released, the third finger is flicked up and over the ball, spinning it somewhere in the direction of gully or fine point. Most leg-spinners will tend to top-spin as well, involving a certain loop in the flight, brought about by the wrist action. The position of the wrist at the moment of delivery decides the type of spin. It is because one has to combine a turn of the wrist with a flick of the third finger along the seam to impart the spin that this is the hardest delivery of all to control.

Leg-spinners are an inaccurate breed and, not surprisingly, become the bane of a captain's life. They are attacking weapons, and in the process may be punished unmercifully. Leg-spin has come to be rather a lost art in England, partly because we have found the finger-spinner to be much more economical for all conditions and more devastating when the conditions help the bowler. The slowness of the wicket makes for less bounce and thus blunts the leg-spinner's knife edge. Overseas the finger-spinner may be economical but is rarely penetrative. Thus the wrist-spinner is given more opportunity, and although he will give plenty of runs away he is always likely to break through. The wickets are harder and faster, the spin will respond quicker and bounce higher, and every English batsman who has played overseas will vouch for the fact that the first two or three outings against a leg-spinner can be disconcerting.

For the budding wrist-spinner who is anxious to learn the three possible types of spin let me try to give him the vital position of the hand.

Whereas the palm of the hand faces the batsman for delivery for a leg-spinner, it faces the ground for delivery for a top-spinner and the fingers no longer point towards the batsman. They point towards mid-on and run practically horizontally to the ground as the ball is flicked out of the hand. In effect, then, the top-spinner leaves the hand a fraction earlier than the leg-spinner.

When we come to the googly it is merely a question of turning the wrist over until the back of the hand is facing the batsman at delivery. From this position the ball is spun in precisely the same way, but it comes up from the third finger, over the top of the little finger, and this you will find spins in the air in the same direction as the off-break.

The value of the googly lies in the element of deception, because the wrist action at the moment of delivery is so fast that it is often quite difficult for the batsman to be sure which it is—a leg-break or a googly. Another virtue of the googly is that it usually comes along slightly slower than a leg-spinner and gains a lot of wickets from batsmen playing a little too early. The googly should be reserved as a surprise packet and not over-used. There are some bowlers who have been clever enough to have a particularly well-concealed googly, and in this case have developed two forms of googly: one that they will show to the batsman quite clearly, bringing about a false sense of confidence, and then, after bowling several of these, they will suddenly pull out their trump card which invariably takes the trick.

Because this form of bowling is so difficult to master, leg-spinners are usually easier to control bowling with the wind. On the other hand, if they are the very slow variety their flight can be particularly teasing, bowling into a wind which is coming up over third man's head. In this way the ball which starts off-stump in the air will drift and tend to pitch round about the leg stump before turning back. The batsman may have moved over a little too far in the first instance and, in consequence, will have to bring the bat back across the line to play the ball—just what the bowler wants to see. Richie Benaud always liked to find the wind helping him in this way and with his unfaltering accuracy he could pose a real problem on his day.

There is no doubt that the allowance of a new ball more frequently has had the effect of pushing the leg-break bowler into the background. Captains prefer to bowl tight in between new balls and let the damage be done by the faster men. This, in turn, reduces the scoring rates and helps to produce the dearth of leg-spinners that we know today. There is nothing so fascinating in cricket as a duel between a top-class batsman and a good leg-spinner. What fun it is to watch a tail-ender swiping and missing, but coming up each ball for more, hoping to clear the fence but knowing that survival is bound to be short-lived! It is the most difficult type of bowling to master, the most attacking type of bowling, and it can be the most exhilarating to play against. I urge the young bowler to be patient as he develops and matures, for he is bound to have many bad days, and I only hope that he will not be so discouraged in the early stages that he does not taste the rewards which will start to come once he has attained a certain measure of accuracy.

Left-arm Bowling

All left-handers start with an advantage because they provide something different. There are so few good left-arm bowlers that batsmen do not get the same opportunities to practice against their type of delivery. It is generally considered that no side is complete without a slow left-arm bowler, and this is most true, of course, under English conditions, where pitches are affected by rain; although, equally, every Australian side touring England has managed very successfully without a slow left-arm bowler. I am sure that the main reason for this lies in the fact that the aspiring slow left-hander in Australia finds it impossible to turn the ball on most wickets he plays on and is nipped in the bud. If the wickets do become wet overseas then it is the medium-paced bowler who makes the inroads.

The slow left-hander has two distinct roles. Because his action, like that of the off-spinner, is so simple and natural, accuracy is his forte. He should be a linchpin for his captain during those long days in the field which every side has to suffer now and again, and should be able to bear the brunt of the work, keeping a check on the scoring.

Flight is one of the fundamentals of good, slow left-arm bowling, especially when the wickets are perfect. But as soon as the wicket shows signs of wear or of responding to spin the slow left-hander should be an attacking weapon, dropping the ball on the spot with ruthless accuracy, taking full advantage of any assistance. He should be bowling round the wicket almost without exception.

The fast or even fast-medium left-arm bowlers are very few and far between and for this reason most captains will welcome them with open arms. I think the two most difficult bowlers I have ever had to bat against were in this category—Bill Johnston of Victoria and Alan Davidson of New South Wales.

In favourable conditions, the left-arm bowler is at his best bowling over the wicket trying to make the ball swing either way. To the right-hand batsman, this can be most disconcerting. A straight ball is still an attacking weapon, bringing the slips and wicket-keeper into play, due to the angle from which it has been bowled. When the ball ceases to swing, however, it may be better for the left-arm bowler to bowl round the wicket as a means of variation.

This covers most of the various techniques and types, but I would like to refer to one or two other aspects of bowling. Two most over-used terms in modern cricket are 'seam' and 'swing'. For some reason, and I have never been given a fully convincing explanation, a cricket ball will swing in the air. Originally we used to play cricket with a two-piece ball, and various exponents of the art of swing made the game a farce because they swung the ball so much. A conference was held and the leather covering is now made out of four pieces. This does not swing so much but helps the spinners a little more. Swing is dependent upon the bowling action—the position of the feet and the position of the hand at the point of delivery. Certain conditions, both pitch and weather, are shown to be desirable for maximum swing to be obtained. A ball with a shiny surface —not necessarily a new ball—in a humid or heavy atmosphere or a wind blowing from the right quarter, will usually lend itself well to a good swing bowler. Yet I have known Alan Davidson, a great exponent of the swinging ball, bowl with a new ball at Melbourne in a heavy atmosphere and he has been unable to swing the ball very much. I find the whole subject highly complex. At the same time I have to concede that the ball does swing and that great bowlers have a considerable measure of control over it.

In delivering the out-swinger a right-hand bowler may occasionally obtain better results by allowing his arm to stray slightly to the right. In fact he is lowering the height of delivery, becoming slightly round-armed; moreover, as the ball leaves the hand, the wrist is turned very slightly so that the palm of the hand moves towards the direction in which the swing is required—for the out-swinger, of course, this would mean in the direction of slip.

When delivering the in-swinger a bowler needs to keep his action as high as possible and the palm of the hand is turned towards the leg side as the ball is delivered. The position of the feet plays a big part in this and in the case of the away-swinger the bowler, like the off-spinner, must put his left foot across the line of the stumps, so as to assist maximum pivot. In direct contrast the in-swinger necessitates an open-chested position, with the left foot splaying out towards the slips.

Swing bowlers should judge the line of the ball so that it will finish on the stumps, after allowing for the swing, so forcing the batsman to play each ball. The greatest crime that new-ball bowlers commit all too often, in every grade of cricket, is that they will continue to bowl enormous swingers at the stumps, with the ball finishing well wide by the time it reaches the batsman. For the captain the sight of such waste is exasperating. The new-ball bowler should aim to pitch the ball up to give it maximum chance of swinging and, in any case, the swinging half-volley is a difficult ball to play with complete safety.

Having said all this, swing, to my mind, is only a quarter of the problem confronting the opening batsmen. It is movement off the pitch which is the most disconcerting thing of all and this is the bare bones of the art of the 'seam' bowler as we have come to term him.

This all starts from the stitching which protrudes from the otherwise flat, spherical surface of a cricket ball. In consequence, the cricket ball is not round. Where the pitch is fast and very hard there will be little deviation, if any, and the art of seam bowling will be nullified. Where there is a highly grassed pitch the seam of the ball can grip the surface and, depending upon the angle of the seam as it lands, so the ball will travel a slightly altered course. Such deliveries will not deviate off the pitch at as sharp an angle as the spinner, but under favourable conditions they will deviate enough to find the edge of the blade and produce mistakes. The real problem to the batsman is that neither he nor the bowler knows when it is going to take place, or which way it is going to turn off the wicket.

The Cutter

This type of delivery belongs to the fast bowlers, who have long, strong fingers, and, consequently, try to spin the ball occasionally as a variation to 'seaming' the ball. One nearly always associates this type of delivery as coming best from very tall men, who use most of their height and strength. At the moment of delivery they flick the seam of the ball with their middle finger, one way or the other, to produce a leg-spin or off-spin. This, clearly, is not spinning the ball, in the same way as the slower bowler imparts spin from the fingers and wrist, but here the first finger cuts across the seam, imparting spin on the ball. Alec Bedser used two different types of grip for his famous leg-cutter—one for dry wickets and the other for wet wickets. For the drier wickets the ball seemed to move very quickly if he cut or spun it off his second finger. To do this the ball was held firmly, but there was no tenseness in the wrist. On rain-affected wickets he held the ball in exactly the same way as the orthodox leg-spinner, but delivered it at his normal pace, cutting or spinning it off the third finger. In this way he was able to achieve more lift off the pitch. The keynote of success lay in the wrist and body action and he would find himself putting more into bowling cutters than into his normal type of delivery. Most important of all for the effectiveness of this delivery is that the ball should be pitched well up to the batsman and bowled at the leg stump with some close catchers waiting on each side of the wicket. Bob Appleyard, the Yorkshire and England bowler, whose great career was cut short by ill-health, was the best exponent I know of the off-cutter. In principle this was exactly the same type of delivery, with the hand and fingers cutting down the other side of the ball.

The great value of this delivery is the speed with which it can be bowled—in fact, it has to be bowled quickly; the quicker it can be bowled the more deviation will be achieved.

The most phenomenal demonstration of the art of cutting the ball in recent years was given by Freddie True-man in the Third Test match at Headingley against Austra-lia in 1961. Here was a slow wicket which did not help the quicker bowlers, and, although it was responsive to spin, slow bowlers Allen and Lock found they were unable to push the ball through fast enough to induce mistakes.

Australia had won the toss and looked to be in an unassailable position, with 187 for two in the first innings, when Freddie Trueman decided to shorten his run and experiment with some off-cutters. In ninety minutes eight Australian wickets fell for 54 runs, Trueman taking five for 20. In the second innings Australia were beginning to ease away again when at 99 for two Freddie Trueman resorted to off-cutters for a second time and in seven overs took six wickets for 5 runs. Alan Davidson had tried to improvise in the same vein and in doing so he presented England with more problems than any other bowler. Here was a set type of conditions made for the cutter where if Alec Bedser could have bowled for both sides the match might have been finished in a day and a half, with neither side making a hundred in any innings.

Variations

Once the bowler has attained a certain degree of accuracy and control he will then be in a position to deceive batsmen with flight and changes of pace. Changes of pace must be slight in order to deceive batsmen into playing the wrong stroke, or even to make them play the correct stroke but too soon or too late. It is important for the bowler to keep the same run-up and the same action—any sort of alteration here tends to give the game away. Peter Loader, of Surrey and England, could produce a most disconcerting slower ball which spun sharply from the off. This, he would assert, took much more out of him than the faster ball, because he would run the full length flat out and put just as much energy into his action. Pitching this slower delivery on a consistent length takes a lot of doing and I am not sure that it is an art which can be taught. It is a knack which one may suddenly hit upon or acquire from watching, maybe, but very difficult, if not impossible, to teach. In this case, however, we are talking of a fast bowler trying to produce a slow ball, which is the most difficult thing of all. It is much more straightforward for the fast bowler to be producing slight variations of his theme and easier still for the slow bowler to produce variations of flight.

I have always felt that too much is made of this phenomena which we refer to as flight. I do not believe that it is a magic which has to be acquired, but rather, I am sure, it is much more straightforward. I think that any good slow bowler who can bowl a good length consistently can develop a natural, teasing flight of his own without having to think about it. He achieves this by straightforward variation of pace, provided he is prepared to give the ball a little bit of air. I am not decrying its value; I think it is a most important part of slow bowling, and, moreover, I do not think it is something magical or inborn. It can come naturally to a slow bowler who uses his wits.

One of the simplest ways of trying to implement some sort of variation is by bowling six identical deliveries, but from six different places around the crease; the first one near the stumps, the second one in the middle of the crease, the third from the extreme edge of the crease. Straight away you have three different angles. The fourth ball, almost a no-ball; the fifth ball three feet from the crease; the sixth ball six feet from the crease, but tossed up. By using the width of the bowling crease and the ground behind the crease you can continue to produce the same mechanical action but alter the length by a different process. This is the cleverest method of producing variation because it is less inclined to upset the bowler's rhythm. It makes for greater accuracy with your intended variation. Variation does not mean six different lengths necessarily. Just as effective are six balls which pitch on the same spot, whilst in flight they all look different.

How does one decide whether to bowl over or round the wicket? Generally speaking, it is the most natural and logical thing to bowl over the wicket and one should only depart from this as an extra form of variation. If the ball is turning sharply the off-spinner will want to go round the wicket to give himself more chance of an l.b.w. decision. The slow left-arm bowler will want to stay round the wicket for this same reason. The only instance for a slow left-arm bowler to bowl over the wicket would arise if he wanted to attack the leg stump. It is not easy for him to bowl round the wicket and attack the batsman's weakness on the leg stump without giving endless runs away down the leg side, because the angle of delivery is naturally straying to leg. But by going over the wicket he straightens up the angle and makes it easier for himself to bowl to his field.

Fitness
Whereas the batsman must be fit to run his singles and to play a long innings, the bowler needs a quite different form of physical fitness. He must have sufficient stamina to withstand long sessions in the field. Once you are fully fit, the task is so much easier and more enjoyable. Full physical fitness makes for mental fitness and helps to produce a confidence which is so essential for success. A bowler will be helped by physical training, but he is going to find the process of bowling such an unusual exercise that the quickest and most satisfactory way of preparing himself for a hard season is by bowling, bowling and more bowling, coupled with spells of fielding.

This is absolutely essential at the start of the season, but there is a danger of overdoing it, for the youngster in

John Snow follows through. He has delivered the ball from close to the stumps and the perfect position of his head suggests accuracy, pace and power.

Sobers caught Cowdrey. Slow off-spinner David Allen bowls round the wicket to Sobers, trying to exploit some of the rough outside the off-stump. The catch will tend to go wide, but here Sobers was as surprised as slip and wicket-keeper to find a faint edge and I had to hurl myself full length to make the chance.

particular, and there are several schools I know who stop their boys bowling in the last few weeks of the summer term, except in the middle. This is a sensible step to curb staleness and reserve the best for the matches.

In an English climate bowlers must take extra care to be well armed with warm pullovers. A hard stint of bowling is usually followed by a spell of standing about in the outfield, asking for the wind to chill the back and bring on stiffness. I am a great believer in taking off all warm clothing whilst one is actually involved in batting or bowling, but the moment one stops to be wrapped in cotton wool.

The feet take the brunt of the knocks for every games player and never get the attention they deserve. Thick socks and well-studded boots with comfortable interiors should be the golden rule of every cricketer.

Bowling is hard work, but with a little care and forethought some of the strain can be eliminated. It is no longer the occupation of the serfs and muscled men; it is now a highly skilled part of the game which requires as much brain as brawn.

F

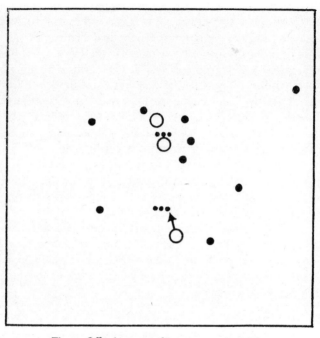

Fig. 1. Off-spinner attacking on a turning wicket

I assume that he is bowling round the wicket; and because every ball is spinning he will want at least five men on the leg side, three in close-catching positions. Slip is always useful for the ball which does not turn as much as expected. If the ball is turning viciously, mid-off should be moved to guard the leg-side boundary wide of mid-on to collect the big hit. A wide mid-off, a cover point and a slip should be sufficient for the off-side. (In first-class cricket, of course, the bowler's limited to five fielders on the leg side.)

The bowler should be able to dispense with mid-off, having a square cover, a wide mid-off and a slip.

If the bowler wants two short legs behind square, then the deep square leg has to come just in front of square.

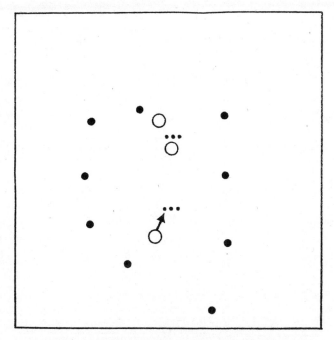

Fig. 2. Field for the off-spinner on a good wicket

Invariably the off-spinner will direct his attack at the off-stump, making the batsman hit him into the covers, or as straight as possible. For this reason the area from extra cover to wide of mid-on should be well manned. Slip and the wicket-keeper become the only attacking fielders as they wait to collect the off-chance.

For the rest it is a question of providing a tight ring to support a spell of good-length bowling. In an emergency, slip can be pushed back to save one behind cover and the square cover can be put on the fence. Mid-off can be pushed back to the boundary.

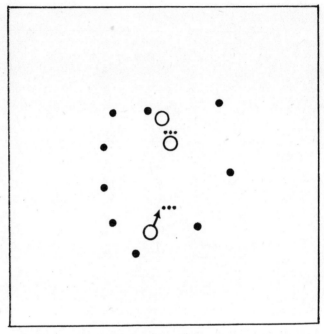

Fig. 3. Field for the slow left-arm spinner on a good wicket

Like the last one, here is a tight off-side ring to support good-length bowling. The bowler is directing his attack at the off-stump and outside; if things begin to get out of hand, mid-off and mid-on can go back to the fence, bringing the other two men on the leg side much straighter. Again, the slip can come out to save the one, pushing square cover back on to the fence. It has to be dire emergency to do without the slip.

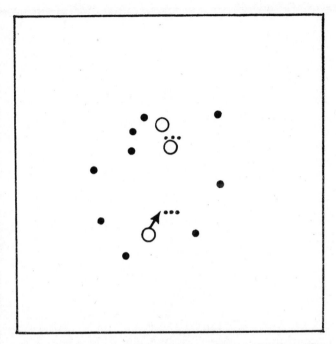

Fig. 4. Field for slow left-arm spinner attacking with the wicket turning

The bowler is directing his attack on the stumps, turning the ball towards the slips, hence the arc of close fielders in that vital area.

With the ball turning a lot away from the bat, I like to see the man behind the wicket on the leg side brought up close for the ball that does not spin so much. If necessary, extra cover can come in close to silly mid-off.

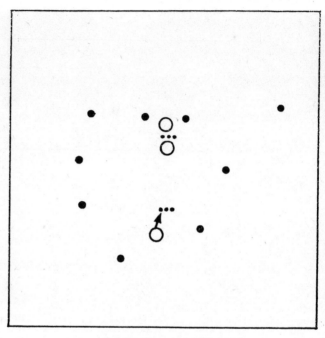

Fig. 5. The leg-spinner on a good wicket

The two vital positions for the leg-spinner are, I think, first slip
for the catch and deep square leg for the bad ball. If he is attacking,
a leg slip is useful for the ball which does not spin or for the googly
which may turn sharply; and one of the off-side ring can come into
the gully.

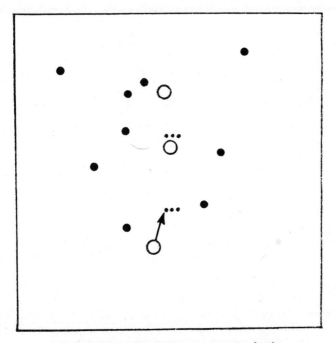

Fig. 6. Field for fast right-arm away-swing bowler

Here is the standard field for this type of bowler—neither all-out attack nor completely defensive.

In attack, third man can come into third slip, long leg into backward short leg, mid-off into the gully and mid-wicket into short square leg.

In defence, second slip can come into extra cover and the gully can strengthen the on-side field between mid-wicket and mid-on. This leaves first slip as the only fielder in a close-catching position.

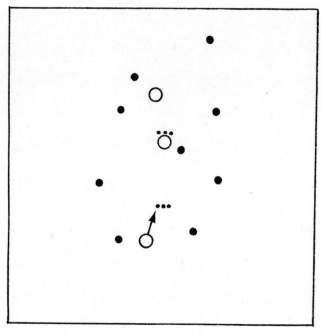

Fig. 7. Field for fast right-arm in-swing bowler

Here we are looking for the ball to be hitting the stumps, collecting an l.b.w. or producing catches in the short-leg area. Slip and gully are always useful positions for the ball which does not swing as much as the batsman expected.

To attack further, fine leg should come in close on the leg side and mid-wicket should come to forward short leg. Even in all-out attack it is a good thing to leave mid-on lurking twenty or thirty yards from the bat for the mishit. Mid-off could be dispensed with and placed on second slip.

In defence the field placing should be very similar to Fig. 6.

Note: only two men are allowed behind the popping crease on the leg side.

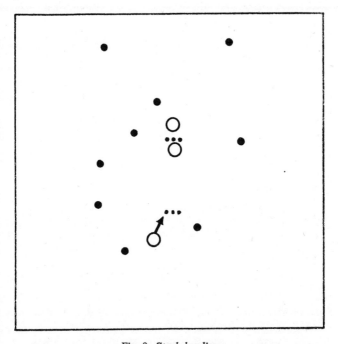

Fig. 8. Stock bowling

This requires a similar field to the fast bowlers' when they are defending. The whole object of the exercise involves a bowler directing his attack one side of the wicket, hoping for the batsman to make mistakes. It is best for the bowler to bowl at the off-stump and outside, and here is the orthodox field. If the bowler is accurate enough, long leg can come up to mid-wicket.

By way of variation I like to see gully put into second slip and third man pushed very square.

Occasionally the bowler will want to attack the leg stump, in which case the gully will come over to backward short leg and the extra cover will go over to a position wide of mid-on, leaving long leg where he is. This will mean five men on the leg side but the bowler must be accurate.

3

FIELDING

FROM the age of five most small boys are throwing a ball against a wall or to each other and in the process they are teaching themselves to become good fielders. A bad fielder cannot really enjoy a reasonable standard of cricket without a feeling of guilt that he is letting the side down. It is half the battle to have speed of foot, agility, balance, a powerful arm and good hands—these are all attributes of the natural games player—but the not-so-gifted are able to work themselves up to a passable standard where they can enjoy their cricket and feel that they are making a worthy contribution to their team. Who will forget Colin Bland or Clive Lloyd on the chase in the outfield, picking up and turning, producing an accurate throw, like a rifle bullet, into the wicketkeeper's gloves above the stumps? Such a sight gives just as much exhilaration as a Hammond drive. You do not necessarily have to be a good runner to excel in the field, for who will forget the facility with which Alan Ealham or Philip Sharpe collect the half-chance without apparent movement? Here, of course, we are considering experts with a natural flair who moved beautifully by instinct.

I always like to quote the case of David Sheppard, tall, angular, somewhat slow on his feet and definitely un-athletic. At the age of sixteen he applied himself to the study of batsmanship so effectively that within three years he was opening the innings for Sussex. This was a remarkable achievement for a man who had really shown no serious signs of becoming a top-class player. Sadly, he was so bad in the field that the captain spent most of the time trying to hide him when, invariably, the difficult catch would find him—and find him wanting. It was soon quite clear to him that unless his fielding improved there was no chance of his earning a place in Test cricket, and indeed it was doubtful whether Sussex could carry him. Typical of the man, he applied himself to the matter assiduously. Within three years he had become a magnificent short-leg or gully fieldsman, using his enormous reach and big hands to good effect, keeping close to the wicket most of the time so as not to expose himself to too much running or throwing. Whilst he played regularly he was as good as any close fielder in the world. This story must surely be an enormous consolation to any outstanding batsman or bowler with ambitions to reach the top who knows himself to be a suspect fielder.

Outfielding

The deep fielder should be a good, fast runner with good hands to cope with high, swirling catches. He must develop an accurate throw. Although the captain will put him in a certain spot—and he should not move from this without permission—he ought to think intelligently and produce suggestions if he feels he is not in quite the appropriate position for the situation. For instance, it is always easier to run in than to run back, so that he should err on the side of being too deep rather than too close. On big grounds he is wasting his time if he stands on the boundary edge, and this is the time when he should ask to come in five or ten yards. He must judge his distance from the batsman, depending, of course, on how far he thinks a full hit will carry, taking the direction of the wind into consideration. At long leg or third man he must place himself so that he can turn two runs into one by moving in with a quick pick-up and throw. He should always be moving in as the ball is bowled, with eye first on the ball and then on the batsman's stroke; if he is intelligent he will soon be anticipating the direction of the stroke and be quick to intercept it.

Beware not to rush into the ball until you have judged the speed, the line and spin, particularly with a high catch. Nothing can be more embarrassing (or more distressing for the bowler) than for a fielder to tear in enthusiastically, only to find the ball sailing overhead. In the case of ground fielding move in towards the ball, lining it up with the back leg, pause, bend, collect, with the back leg acting as a second line of defence, and in one movement transfer the weight from the back foot on collection to the front foot with the throw. On collecting the ball, try to turn the back towards the wicket, left shoulder leaning, as if you were playing a cover drive, to help towards an accurate aim. Over-arm rather than the flat, low throw is best and is less likely to cause an injury. So many people throw their arms out through a jerky, low flick, without any proper follow-through.

With high catching, obviously, judgement is the first essential, so that you get your feet in the right place with the weight on the toes, waiting for the catch. The hands should be held high, so that your eye is kept on the ball right into the hands; then the hands relax as they close on to the ball, bringing them into the chest with the weight sagging and relaxing on to the heels.

There are three types of throw. From thirty to forty yards most good outfielders will propel the ball from boundary to stumps without any need to give it much arc in the flight, but over forty yards you have to allow for a certain trajectory. If you are going for a run-out from fifty yards or more it is then better to aim to bounce the ball once on its way to the stumps, and in dry conditions you can skid the ball through, to gather pace off the ground. Where the outfield is soft or very wet this is impracticable, but, sadly, this is a method that is dying out and should be revived, I feel.

Deep fielding is easy to practise and great fun. A good batsman, wielding the bat to a ring of six or seven outfielders, with first some ground fielding straight to the man, interspersed with some ground fielding wide of the man—the names being called out by the batsman—then some high catches, first direct and then involving a run, then some lower-trajectory catches, which you might experience at deep mid-off. Then the fielders ought to come close to the batsman and have the ball hit up high over their heads so that they have to turn and run fifteen yards away from the striker. All the time the wicket-keeper should be standing at a stump a few yards away from the batsman, allowing the fielders to practise every length and type of throw. A half-hour session with six fielders is good exercise, very entertaining and first-class practice.

Close Fielding

Every cricketer should feel comfortable, wherever he is put in the field. The youngster, then, should not specialize too early until he has tried out every position on the field. It won't be very long before he realizes that there is more to close fielding than he knew before. There is nothing more humbling to an all-round games player, who thinks he has a good eye and can catch everything, than to find himself dropping the simplest parabola snicked to first slip.

To the genius like Sobers there is no need for rules—just a little concentration and his natural skill will do the rest for him. But more ordinary mortals need practice, experience and to obey certain self-made rules. There comes a time when specialization is important, though not to the extent when the slightest alteration might let the side down. Yet it is quite extraordinary how good slip fielders often find it difficult to be quite so successful at short leg, and vice versa. Apparently Wally Hammond disliked fielding at short leg, whilst Tony Lock, who must be the greatest leg slip in all history, found that the slips on the off-side caused real problems. Strange! Let us try to analyse the position and establish some golden rules.

Keep the hands hard with constant practice and yet loose and pliable when catching. Always begin practice with an old ball, because it is softer. You will find that the first half a dozen catches will sting more than usual because it takes a few moments for Nature's juices to bring about that puffiness which acts as a protective cover inside of the hand. The most dangerous thing one can do is to start off with a hard new ball and throw it about too violently. This is when one is most prone to injury and the hands are not conditioned to take the full knocks. After a little while one can feel the hands warming, and somehow they appear to expand, instilling confidence. This is why fielding in wet, cold conditions is such a nightmare. You may go through the motions before the start of play, warming the hands through, but after an hour of inactivity they have assumed their rather defenceless condition again. For this reason I always allow my close fielders to put their hands in their pockets on cold days, although it does look slovenly as a general principle. I urge my fielders to clap their hands together frequently, so as to keep them warm and the juices circulating.

Grab the ball between overs and hurl it around amongst yourselves, three or four times quickly—anything, in other words, to give your catching machinery a better chance. Without warm hands, in perfect condition, catching is doubly hard and highly dangerous, and you cannot give full support to the bowler.

Weight should be evenly distributed, leaning forward on to the balls of the feet, hands loose, relaxed and ready, legs comfortably apart and the balance coiled, ready to spring in any direction. Just as the batsman is about to play the stroke you should be motionless. Concentration is vital, but it is insufficient merely to be alert and keen if your mind is not fixed to a more positive purpose. So many close fielders, with every attribute for doing the job perfectly, fall down because they tend to gaze hopefully at the general scene instead of focussing on the point where the ball leaves the edge of the bat. First slip and leg slip should always watch the ball from the moment it leaves the bowler's hand and should assume that it will be deflected off the bat in their direction. Just as the wicket-keeper assumes that every ball is for him, assume each ball is yours, however improbable it may seem from the direction of the ball bowled or the type of stroke. If you study the great close fielders you will often see them anticipating where a catch might have gone in spite of the fact that the batsman has struck the ball away quite safely.

Second slip and backward short leg can watch the ball from the bowler's hand, although I prefer them to forget

about the bowler and the pitch, but to keep their eye glued
not merely to the bat but to the very edge of the bat. Just
as the stroke is being played you get a feel of how high the
ball is bouncing and your eye can only shift up or down the
bat edge. This, then, is what we mean by concentration
—focussing the eye on a specific point at the moment of
impact. If you do this successfully you graduate out of that
awful state where you are conscious of a red blur and the
noise of the dreaded click to a confident fielder, who seizes
on to the picture of the ball leaving the edge of the bat
before you hear any noise. The quicker you sight the ball,
the quicker you move, the sooner you relax the hand for
pouching the ball. Most dropped catches have been seen
too late for sufficient relaxation—and this is why a good
fielder makes a difficult catch look easy.

The gully is a difficult position because you have to be
prepared for angled snicks as well as powerful blows off the
full face of the bat. This requires courage and extra concentration. It is most difficult to keep the eye focussed when
the bat is being waved with a flourish. In fact, it is much
safer to keep calm and still with a violent stroke, because
the quicker one can see the ball, the quicker one can dodge
for safety if need be.

The short-leg position is different in that you cannot keep
your eye focussed on the inside edge of the bat for the very
good reason that the bat is hidden from view until the
moment of impact. The best short-leg fielders I have known
have kept their eye focussed to a point round about the
batsman's front knee. Whatever movement the batsman
embarks upon, the fielder remains crouching and gazing
intently at this one point, only prepared to switch the focus
on seeing the bat come through.

On analysis, given a certain basic, sound position where

Clive Lloyd is the most exciting outfielder in the world today.
Here the ball comes on his wrong side, but so perfect is his
balance he will gather and be able to throw on the turn to either
end. A menace to batsmen.

A misjudgement by Ian Chappell and Alan Knott shows no
mercy with a lightning stumping. Matchless concentration, speed
of eye, hand and feet and boundless enthusiasm.

the weight is nicely balanced, the key to success lies in a stillness which allows the eye the best possible view. From this point on it is then just a matter of reflex action, but the sooner this is triggered off the more effective the result.

Background plays a big part. On a nice, bright day a shining red ball will loom up clearly out of a white background or a particularly green tree. But on a dull day a dirty ball will be camouflaged against the brown trunk of a tree, grey seating or the brickwork of a house in the distance.

I can still feel a hollow in my stomach today when a beautiful away-swinger from Freddie Trueman collected the edge of MacMorris's bat and at that very fraction of a second I caught a glimpse—a vivid picture—of the ball flying high to my left hand. It was going to be a nasty catch, travelling very fast, but my concentration had given me a good start and there was a fifty-fifty chance of success. The ball climbed steeply from the ground and suddenly disappeared into the background of the pavilion just beneath the England balcony. My tummy seemed to drop away from me, and just as I was about to panic the ball came back into view again, thanks to an enormous white marquee which could be seen through the archway made by the pavilion and the members' stand. I shot up my left hand in desperation and was able to knock the ball up and, fortunately, all was well again. Background is something one can do nothing about, of course, but before you are too hard on yourself for the two or three catches you may drop —you cannot make this an excuse to the bowler!—you can console yourself that things could have been easier for you.

Don't set yourself too high a standard or else you are

G

doomed to disappointment. If you catch two out of three that will be well above average.

You will find that one hand will be stronger than the other. Aim to catch as much as possible with both hands —only one hand in an emergency. In practice try and catch all the time in your weak hand and you will be surprised how quickly this will improve. I have a small and particularly weak left hand, but have practised with it for a long time now. What a thrill it was, going full length at Leeds one day, to catch Alan Davidson with my left hand only, and although I shall never be fully confident with it, I do know that it has a fifty-fifty chance of success, which would never have come about without persistent practice. I try to block out my left hand as much as possible by having an agreement with my fellow slips. I field a lot at second slip and like to stand closer to first slip than perhaps I need, with the understanding that he can go for everything to his right—assuming that he is right-handed. I will then go for everything about the line of my left foot with both hands. To my right I will push third slip farther away than he may want to stand, but on the understanding that I will make ground to cover that area. If first slip is particularly agile and confident he will often push me away into a normal position, with the understanding that he will be prepared to dive a long way to his right. In this way, then, one can have team-work among close fielders—quite a lot of fun and all most helpful to the bowlers.

Confidence plays such a big part in all this. Two or three dropped catches in close succession brings one's morale down to rock bottom and no amount of practice can give one sufficient confidence for catching the fourth. By dropping the fourth and fifth you are on the edge of a nervous breakdown and will be tempted to appeal to the captain for a move into the deep field. This is where an astute captain's firm hand can put it all right. Eventually, you will catch a 'blinder', just when you least expect it. The nightmare is over and before very long you are back in a confident groove again, hoping for the chances to come your way.

4

WICKET-KEEPING

AT THE age of ten I thought I was just about the best wicket-keeper in the world except for the young Godfrey Evans, who was that bit bigger and more experienced! I adored wicket-keeping because I felt I was in the game with every ball bowled.

When I was eleven I made the great mistake of producing a googly under my headmaster's eye and from that moment onwards the gloves were denied me for ever. Consequently, I have always taken a great deal of interest in the art of wicket-keeping and in the various champions I have met. Strange to relate, I have come to know three great England wicket-keepers very well indeed. George Duckworth was scorer and baggage master on four tours, and he became almost a father to me; I played my first county match for Kent with Leslie Ames as my captain and since then we have come to know each other very closely. I do not know how many times I have fielded slip next to Godfrey Evans and Alan Knott, both for Kent and for England. So, then, if I am not fully qualified to talk on wicket-keeping myself I feel I have had sufficient personal contact with the subject to pass on a few thoughts.

What special requirements does the job call for, having assumed, of course, that you have the natural ability of any

good games player? First you must have courage, for few
men have stood behind the stumps for very long without
suffering a severe knock. In the primitive days their gloves
were poor protection, and you only have to meet a pensioned-
off wicket-keeper to see what his gnarled fingers thought
about it all. Today gloves are well padded, with rubber
finger-stalls and cleverly devised inner gloves—we have
come a long way since the days when George Duckworth
used to put a fillet steak in the palm of each hand to soften
the blows from Harold Larwood. In those days first slip
was not the most enviable position to be standing in on a
hot Australian summer's day, not because of the speed of
the catches but the stench which surrounded Duckworth!

The modern wicket-keeper dives about much more than
his counterpart thirty years ago. Thus it is important for
him to have good, strong gloves and very light pads. His
hands are going to take a lot of knocks, but nothing must
restrict his movement. Godfrey Evans once told me that
wicket-keeping pads are an admission of failure and that
on good wickets he could have done without them altogether. What's more, I believe he could have done, but I
don't advise anyone else to try the experiment.

Whilst the bowler is marking out his run, most wicket-
keepers will be drawing a line from which to stand. This will
vary according to the pace of the bowler and the bounce in
the wicket. I was always intrigued by the way that Godfrey
Evans would mark a line eighteen inches from the stumps
just before he took his first ball from a slow bowler. For
each delivery he would be crouched, leaning slightly towards
the wicket, weight on toes, clear of the off-stump, so that
he had a good view of the ball and was poised very still,
like a leopard waiting to spring. Nothing could suppress his
energy or enthusiasm, the by-products of peak fitness.

To the ball wide of the off-stump he tried to move over far enough so that the left hand would take most of the impact. By covering the extra ground a thick edge would have a chance of deflecting into the right glove. Furthermore, this method gave his right hand freedom to roam, should the ball ricochet on to the batsman's pad and present an opportunity of a scooping catch.

In exactly and precisely the same way he would move over down the leg side, aiming to take the ball in the right hand, with the left hand free to operate wheresoever it was needed. This was the main reason why he was able to bring off some miraculous leg-side catches. Standing up to the wicket meant that he was able to take cleanly some deliveries which most wicket-keepers would have clutched at in vain. But it did mean that he was credited with certain snicked dropped catches, which would have escaped other wicket-keepers, but only he was brilliant enough to turn them into chances. True, first slip would be denied possible chances occasionally, but on the whole it is better for the wicket-keeper to take them, if possible, as so often that particular catch is the horror which tends to fly to first slip's left hand and present a fearful proposition. Like the good slip fielder, he assumes that every ball is going to go through to him and never, never, never anticipates that the batsman will hit the ball in the direction he intends. This must be a permanent golden rule.

We hear an awful lot about hands—good, safe hands—when we talk about wicket-keepers, but this is putting the cart before the horse. In the first place it needs quick footwork to bring the hands into such a position in time to make the taking of the ball look easy. The incidentals of wicket-keeping—such as whether or not to go for slip catches, whether to stand up or back, when or how to adjust one's position to a particular type of bowler—these must all be learnt the hard way, by experience and by watching others.

The three most essential functions that a wicket-keeper must perform, and so contribute to the success of his team, lie in his assistance to the captain, his assistance to the bowlers and his assistance to the fielders.

From his position he sees what the bowler is doing, how the wicket is playing and how the batsman is shaping. With this information he should become a hive of information for his captain and, without being a nuisance or demanding a set course of action, he should offer suggestions. He should become guide, philosopher and friend to his captain. In just the same way he can assist each bowler in turn. He can help his captain most of all by boosting the bowlers' morale, if and when their confidence starts to waver. But most important of all the great wicket-keeper will, through intervention, cover up bad throwing by moving into positions where the casual spectator will not realize there has been anything amiss. There is nothing more stimulating to the team in the field than good, sharp ground fielding and throwing. Two bad throws in succession can undermine the pressure which the bowlers are trying to create and the wicket-keeper can play a vital part in clinching the process.

I always feel sorry for the wicket-keeper who, in his enthusiasm, seeks for much-needed practice by standing behind the batsman in a practice net. So rarely is there sufficient room for him to do this and often the state of the wickets make it difficult for him to get safe, realistic practice. Again, the batsmen tend to be more adventurous in nets, producing a type of stroke that they would never consider in the middle.

Nothing produces efficiency quicker than endless practice, but a wicket-keeper's lot in this direction is extremely difficult. It is always worth going into a net without a batsman, leaving one stump up rather than three, and if this is not completely realistic, at least he is getting the confidence of feeling a ball hit the middle of the gloves. As the wicket-keeper is such an integral part of all fielding practice, obviously this is good for him, but there is no easy way for him to practise behind the stumps, other than in match play.

Alan Knott is a very helpful and never-ending source of information to the captain. Moreover, he can be of great encouragement to bowlers, especially if they are not quite in their best form. A wicket-keeper can play a vital role as psychologist, lifting his bowlers with a friendly rallying call every now and again or, indeed, with a suggestion about a weakness. He should try to make himself, in a quiet way, the most important man on the field.

5

COACHING AND PRACTICE

CRICKET presents such difficulties because batting is such an unnatural occupation. Hockey and golf and squash involve a natural swing of the arm. For the batsman the square cuts and the hooks, the hits to the leg side, are all natural strokes, but playing with a straight bat either in defence or attack demands an unnatural movement.

In the cases of Don Bradman or Garfield Sobers or Denis Compton, to mention just three of the great players, they taught themselves, but the average games player does need coaching to become a proficient batsman. There are not many who can get far without assistance.

Overseas the wickets are so uniform in bounce and pace that it is easier for the schoolboy to grow in skill and confidence. In this country the varying surfaces make it a different story. The Englishman are coached from an early age and tend to become too stilted. We are always being accused of over-coaching our youngsters. Watch a Test match between England and Australia and you do not have to be told which players have been coached along orthodox lines and which have been left a greater degree of freedom. In contrast, watch some overseas player floundering on an awkward pitch in England and you will see the English player making more of a fist of it. The answer lies in achieving a happy medium, and to this end depends the skill of a good coach. The best coaches have recognized the true and vital natural potential of their pupils and will not baulk it. They will endeavour to harness all that to a basic technique which everyone must acquire at some stage. Most intelligent schoolboys will imitate their idols, and here again the coach can encourage certain things but must point out the dangers involved. The coach, therefore, is at his best in a positive role rather than acting as an influence which suppresses originality or enterprise merely for the sake of pandering to orthodoxy. If any player has an unorthodox stroke which brings success more often than not it must be wrong to stop it. It is best, then, to help the batsman see clearly the degree of risk and the chances of success.

The coach is powerless without good practice wickets and so often the people charged with the responsibility of running cricket grounds around the countryside just do not take the trouble to prepare surfaces with sufficient care and attention. Many young players have had their confidence shaken by a nasty injury. How can one stop a youngster backing away if a ball is likely to fly? Attractive stroke players are produced from good, fast, true wickets where they can learn the fundamentals in safety, and there is no substitute for a good, true, turf wicket. If this cannot be found then a hard, artificial pitch is the next-best thing.

You cannot take too much care as you seek to provide the best possible practice conditions. There are two distinct attitudes of mind in approaching a practice session. The England team will arrive for a practice session the day before a Test match merely for a 'loosener'. They may have been playing cricket for six or seven weeks without a break and the last thing they want is practice. Yet it is valuable

that they should practise at the ground on the day before
the match. A casual spectator might be horrified at their
haphazard approach to a big match. I always feel it is bad
publicity for the game when England players do not take
the net practice seriously, yet in this instance there is a very
good case for them to relax a little.

For the most part I like to see cricketers taking their nets
seriously, in the same frame of mind as if they were playing
in the middle. If everybody is giving of their best, practice
will give pleasure and prove worth while. Most batsmen
apply themselves for a short while until their concentration flags; then a few careless slogs can reduce the bowler's
enthusiasm and a practice session which started seriously
degenerates, to the detriment of all concerned.

After all, the secret of success in any department of the
game is in concentration and application. Of course, you
must enjoy your cricket, and particularly your practice
sessions, but, best of all, let the enjoyment come from a good
performance, assisted by quiet and determined concentration. The coach can create this atmosphere by setting each
individual a target and inspiring him to achieve that little
bit extra. Where there is no coach available each individual
can set himself certain standards. I have always batted in
a net as if it were a match, imagining the possible field
positions. Occasionally I would forsake the match conditions in order to perfect certain strokes or to eradicate a
particular weakness and in these circumstances you need
to concentrate fully on that objective. But there is no better
practice than playing in a net under a self-imposed discipline of playing under match conditions.

The assiduous approach to practice by Bob Appleyard,
Yorkshire and England, was a perfect example of how to
make the maximum use of net practice. He would always

bowl as though it were the final Test match, with you the last man in and this the last ball of the match, with several thousand pounds hanging on the result. In consequence you were always fully stretched—ideal if you were looking for good practice. On the 1954 tour of Australia Bob and I were both rested for a match and during our week off I had five twenty-minute net innings against him. We played it seriously on each occasion, with an imaginary field set and altered by him. I don't remember him bowling me out, because the conditions were all in my favour—he could have had me caught a couple of times—but I rather doubt whether I made double figures in more than three hours' batting. Such was the concentration, I almost got to the state where I imagined the crowd's slow hand-clap!

Derek Underwood is very much the same. Alan Knott works very hard in practice, of course, and Geoff Boycott would spend all day and every day batting in the nets if he could find the bowlers.

Personally, I don't think you can overdo practice provided you can maintain concentration. Once that slackens, then I think you are wasting energy and time and the seeds of staleness can set in. Above all, make practice fun.

6

CAPTAINCY

I URGE every young cricketer to set his heart on becoming captain of his school team. It will stimulate a completely fresh approach to the game which he will never regret. At junior-school level, of course, one is not experienced enough to be anything more than a pawn in the schoolmaster's game, nor has one the bowlers at one's command to be able to manipulate and steer the game, but one has to start somewhere. There is no short cut to gaining experience of this kind.

Given all the experience and skill in the world it then depends upon the strength and balance of the bowling attack under your command. The best general is lost without the right kind of troops for the battle.

Stuart Surridge, who captained Surrey in their successful five-year spell in the early 'fifties, was a very fine leader of a great side. He had the happy knack of getting the most out of the very considerable resources and for that reason he was a great captain. He would be the first to admit that as captain of Leicestershire over those same years he would not have come out of it quite so well.

Bowlers win matches, not batsmen; bowlers control the game of cricket, and it is to the bowling strength that the wise captain first looks when he is assessing his side's possibilities. A glance at the County Championship table will very quickly show which sides have the best bowling combinations. The teams in the top half of the table secure more wickets than those lower down and the performances of batsmen are relatively less important. So then in the final analysis the eventual success or failure of a captain will be dependent on the return his bowlers can give him.

Having established that fact, what are the attributes that make him a good captain? First of all, he must have such a mind that will be quick to adapt itself to the ever-changing pattern for which cricket is so famous. It is not essential that he be the best batsman or bowler in the team, but that is of enormous help; it is not essential for him to be the most experienced player of the team, but, again, it makes life easier for him if he is; it is not essential for him to be an all-rounder, although it is of obvious help to the side to be able to contribute at all points of the game and it enables him, as captain, to be in the centre of things as much as possible, where he can lead by example. Also, by being both batsman and bowler, he is more likely to understand the changing moods and feelings of his men as they come under the varying pressures. The good captain is one who has taken time and care to understand his colleagues and the little things which make one tick and another falter, who knows when a reprimand will spur one man on and when it would be the worst possible treatment for another.

In other words, the captain is seeking to get each member of his team to produce his best all the time. This is not always going to be possible, of course, because a man's temperament is the most complicated phenomena to predict or to handle.

There are four distinct responsibilities which the captain has to shoulder. First the selection of the team and preparation for the big match; second, captaining the side from the pavilion as a member of the batting side; third, captaining in the field; and last, but not least, the manner in which he and his side conduct themselves in victory or defeat.

In picking the best side one aims for a perfect balance. The captain must first of all choose four full bowlers, regardless of their batting ability; a balance of two quick bowlers and two spinners for preference, and the spin bowlers of contrasting styles. England have chosen two off-spinners in several Test matches recently because they are the two best spin bowlers in the country, but by doing so the captain's lot has been a very dull one, and there are times when we have sighed for variation. Choose the best wicket-keeper, again regardless of batting ability.

Now turn to the batting, thinking first of two opening batsmen, a left-hander and right-hander combination for preference. Then, obviously, the three best stroke players will occupy the positions three, four and five. There is now one position open—number six—and before this gap can be filled the captain must assess whether there is a fifth bowler to be found from the five batting places he has filled. He may find there are two useful change bowlers who could support his main combination of four; in this case he can allot the number six position to the next-best batsman. If amongst his top five batsmen none of them can bowl at all he will have to pick an all-rounder for number six, with the emphasis upon bowling. To pick a full bowler for this position makes the attack rather lop-sided in favour of the bowlers, and he can only afford this situation if his wicket-keeper is a high-class batsman. Here, then, and only in this instance, can he think again about the wicket-keeper and choose him with his batting ability in mind. This is playing with fire.

The first England team I played in comprised five full batsmen, four full bowlers, all-rounder Trevor Bailey at number six and wicket-keeper Godfrey Evans at number seven. It was a good and effective combination, but the strain on the five batsmen was intense. Ideally, the captain must aim for six full batsmen, one of whom can be counted as a full bowler (or two more than useful change bowlers). This is where the Australians have always had better-balanced sides than ours. Davidson, Benaud, Simpson and Greg Chappell are all batsmen/bowlers—making the task of the selectors so much easier. The West Indians of 1963 were a stronger combination for having Sobers and Worrell, two of their main batsmen, who could be relied upon to bowl—both, incidentally, able to bowl either quick or slow.

In selecting his side the captain must not forget the value of fielding. It is all too easy to sit down and pick the best team without any good, specialist fielders who can catch close to the bat. I have known an England team include an experienced high-class slip fielder whose batting was below full Test class.

Having arrived at the best permutation, the captain must see that the team come to the post physically fit and confident. I am not a great believer in physical training as a help to cricket fitness, although I can see its value for fast bowlers. I believe that practice, practice and more practice alone can produce the right amount of fitness that you want for bowler and batsman alike. It is valuable for a batsman to have sufficient batting practice against each type of bowler; it is helpful for the bowlers to try out their full run in the middle as well as in the nets, and it is worth going to the trouble of practising in the middle. It is essential for everybody to have some outfield practice, including high catches and long throwing; it is vital for all the close catchers to have their hands hardened by constant short sessions, with five or six around the man with the bat. Catches off the bat are by far the most valuable practice, because they encourage the fielder to watch the ball leave a particular point off the bat. On the morning of a match each member of the team should be out on the ground, throwing the ball about, having a short knock and a few catches, whilst the captain is studying the pitch, tossing and fulfilling the various pre-match duties that have to be undertaken.

Usually the captain will want to win the toss for his side and bat, but one can never lay down any hard-and-fast rules as to why and when this should be otherwise. Sometimes the wicket will look as if it would be of considerable help to the bowlers early on, before drying out into a wonderful batting surface. Here is the ideal opportunity, with the right bowlers, to insert the opposition and bargain on an early break-through. The scene is then set for one's own batsmen to be romping home against a smallish total when the conditions have improved. This situation usually applies to dry weather and hardish wickets, where either morning dew or over-watering in the wicket preparation has left a degree of moisture in the surface.

With regard to wickets which seem 'tailor-made' for spin bowlers, these tend to deteriorate as the match progresses and here it is always best to bat first.

There is a third set of conditions where the wicket is perfect and shows no sign of deteriorating but one has a weak bowling side. The captain is then justified in putting the opposition in to bat, hoping for a fair declaration and trusting that his batsmen will win the match for him, chasing a target against the clock.

Occasionally we can use the defensive insertion, where the

H

captain sees that there is going to be some early life in the wicket and fears the strength of the opposition opening bowlers. Much better to be bowling himself, even without great success, than to expose his own batsmen to a certain grilling and a disaster from which he has little chance of recovery.

These are just a few generalities, though one could go on quoting more detailed instances for ever.

Let us assume that we have won the toss and are going to bat. The captain has set the batting order—and batsmen like to get used to a set position. The openers consist of a right-hander and left-hander, both of them good runners between the wickets and, moreover, quick to push the good-length ball away into gaps in such a manner that they make singles rather than sitting back waiting for them to come. The captain must badger his team constantly to keep looking for this quick single. Here is one aspect of the game which we all tend to become lazy about. The captain must see that each of his batsmen takes the trouble to play themselves in, sensibly and quietly, but at some stage they must make a positive bid to assume the offensive role. Of course, the captain must not over-interfere with the techniques of his players, but he is shirking his duty if he does not keep chasing up the various little points which tend to be forgotten. In drawing up his batting order he will expect the bulk of his runs to come from numbers one to five, with perhaps number five or six being a solid type of batsman who can act the sheet-anchor role in an emergency. He then needs to have a couple of quick-scoring tail-enders up his sleeve if the situation demands action just prior to a declaration, or should he be chasing a target in the dying moments of a game. It is always difficult for the captain to be giving advice to his batsmen from the pavilion, but they do need instructions, from time to time, as to how the captain is viewing the situation. It is certainly much better for the players themselves to be over-informed than to be kept in the dark.

The captain's task really begins in the field. He must decide which end is going to suit each particular bowler and he must have in his mind's eye three types of field to be set for each bowler. At first he will employ the completely attacking field, where runs are of no consequence and the only object is to keep up the pressure; later he can fall back on the half-way field where the bowler is attacking the stumps, and yet on the boundary edge third man and long leg have been placed to save fours; nevertheless, there are several people in catching positions. Then he may have to resort to the third and completely defensive field, where runs have to be saved at all costs and a wicket will only come from the batsman's error.

The captain then has to try to find out, as tactfully as he can, which ends the bowlers would prefer, but he must not promise too much, in case all the bowlers prefer one end! But it is a great help if he knows their preferences, so that when one tires, the second with a preference for that end can be changed round to give him every chance. Having juggled with the ends, so as to keep each bowler as happy as it is possible to do, the field setting for each situation is then a policy decision according to the circumstances. And here the bowler and captain can clash. The bowler may have a plan and is confident of success, granted certain field positions, but the captain may feel the time has come to relinquish all-out attack for complete defence for a few overs. The ultimate decision needs a firm and tactful hand. There are two ways of doing it. On the one hand there is the old-fashioned Peter May-like overruling which brooks no argument. Alternatively, there is the more modern trade-union system of consultation, but where the successful captain gets his own way nine times out of ten! This is the 'What do you think, but, obviously, this is how we are going to do it' way! Not quite as bad as that, of course, but one has to suit one's conversational tactics to the bowler's temperament.

The captain in the field has to spur his men on, stop them from wandering from the positions in which they were placed, encourage those who are finding it hard going, but stamp on laziness in no uncertain terms. The unfortunate fielder who drops a catch is always a difficult one to deal with and a vital question presents itself. Was he asleep or was he trying too hard? And, depending on your verdict, two quite different forms of treatment are to be applied. For the most part one must be generous, because no one drops a catch on purpose.

The captain is responsible for seeing that his team behave themselves properly on and off the field. After all, this is a game, not a business; it is a game governed by certain laws, which can be eluded by any rogue who sets out to do so; it is controlled by umpires who are human—and there are more impartial ones than cheats—although I guarantee if one were to take a survey of batsmen's complaints between eight o'clock and ten o'clock on a Saturday evening throughout the country inns of England one would not think very much of the skill and integrity of English umpiring! This is perhaps the most difficult task for a captain—a responsibility which he would gladly do without—and one which he has to oversee in the quietest possible way.

Sir Donald Bradman told me once that when he was captain of Australia his mind was alerted to the task every waking hour of his life. He did not find it a chore or a burden, but fascinating and enjoyable. He accepted it as a way of life. Clearly, the school or club captain is not going to be so dedicated, but certainly within the hours of play one should hope for something of this feeling. You will be proved wrong on so many occasions; you will learn not to be dogmatic about any aspect of the game; you will learn to be tolerant and understanding of one's colleagues; you will come to see that cricket is the most difficult game to master or control, even for the greatest player.

One thing is certain: that everyone with the chance of captaining a side should seize it with enthusiasm. I guarantee he will be absorbed by its varied interest. Provided he is not too ambitious, and realizes that at times he will feel like the dog who is chasing his tail and can never quite get hold of it, he will find it all thoroughly enjoyable and rewarding.

The hardest job for the captain is to be able to make quick decisions and then have the courage of his convictions. He must be able to view a situation, assimilating all the facts, and then be prepared to take prompt action.

When to close an innings often presents a delicate problem requiring fine judgement. The risk of losing must be balanced against the chances of victory. It is a matter of how much time the captain is going to allow his bowlers to dismiss the opposition. In this appraisal the relative skills of the teams and the state of the wicket must be taken into consideration. We can all quote instances where the target set has been outrageously high and the captain concerned has been blamed for his over-cautious attitude, but I shall never forget the day at Southampton when I set Hampshire 320 to make in six hours on a good wicket. They were a good batting side, if not outstanding, but they possessed two brilliant stroke makers, Colin Ingleby-Mackenzie and Roy Marshall. Unfortunately for me, these two brilliant batsmen chose this day, of all days, to excel themselves, and they won the match for Hampshire with an hour to spare. Had we dismissed Mackenzie and Marshall cheaply, they would probably never have looked like reaching the target. If our bowlers had not been able to break through I might have been accused of setting too high a figure for them in a last innings of a county match. Such are the difficulties, and it is always easy to be wise after the event.

There are captains who overwork their fast bowlers at the start of the day and burst them early on. Others take them off at regular intervals, regardless of whether they are being successful or not. One thing is certain: the fast bowlers respond better to short spells so that they are left with sufficient reserve to recapture their zip after a short breather. The only time the captain is justified in bursting them is when he has established an early advantage and wants to push it home.

Generally speaking, frequent bowling changes are a sound policy, for apart from the rest it brings to the bowler, it is continually presenting the batsmen with something new. This does not always suit the slow bowler, who likes to forge a plan which may take several overs to work through. Nothing is more infuriating for him than the restless captain who breaks up his little plot half-way through. This is a very real instance where captaincy by consultation is absolutely essential.

The greatest test of a captain's ability is whether he is capable of anticipating a batsman's weakness. How often do we see a player making a bad mistake and the field change being made too late. This is shutting the door after the horse has bolted, and all too seldom does a second chance occur after the batsman has had his warning. If and when the captain can sense it coming the fieldsman is there in good time. Skilful field placing is a most vital aspect of captaincy. It is certainly the best way to a bowler's heart, especially a youngster's, for nothing can destroy his morale quicker than careless field placing. The batsman is allowed to escape and the demoralized bowler loses any confidence he once had. I am all for giving a bowler a protective field to save him from punishment at the outset, so that he can build his confidence. In this way he is given a few moments to establish himself, producing his wiles from a position of strength.

The captain in the field has three problems permanently on his mind:

1. Is the field placing just right?
2. Does the bowler need a rest?
3. Does the pitch call for a different form of attack?

These are always going to be imponderables and the restless captain is never going to be wholly satisfied whatever happens.

Sir Leonard Hutton was my first England captain and he made a deep impression upon me. He has so many critics that I go out of my way to record my loyalty to all that was so good about him.

Peter May combined the attributes of being a very good batsman, a good fielder and a likable man, with a good knowledge of the game. His was a quiet but firm regime.

Richie Benaud had all the qualities to make a fine captain and he would be one of the few bowlers who have not been criticized for not under-bowling or over-bowling himself. This is a very real problem for a bowler captain.

Finally I believe that Frank Worrell, who tragically died so young, was the most complete all-round captain that the game of cricket has known. He was a natural leader; he always had the complete confidence of every team he captained because of his exceptional knowledge of the game and his thorough understanding of his men. He was also, of course, a superb player, and I am convinced that the playing ability of a captain counts for a very great deal.

7

THINKING AHEAD

I HAVE tried to give you some insight into the basic principles. Let us stand outside the game for a while and take a
broader view.

As each year goes by more and more concentrated
thought goes into top-class sport. In athletics and swimming
the clock can prove the increasing technical skills. In the
team games it is impossible to make measurements. One
can only use judgement and compare, say, Nastase with
Fred Perry, a Cup Final at Wembley twenty years ago
with last year's final, or the field placing that was set to
Bradman against the pattern as it is today.

There is no doubt that application, physical fitness and
tactical strategy have all been transformed and the game
has been lifted. In consequence, the general standard has
levelled out and fewer stars shine so brightly. This results in
less dramatic theatre, less exciting box office appeal, and
induces a tendency to wail the age-old cry 'The game is not
what it used to be'. This is false, anyway as far as technical
advancement is concerned.

The result of more top-class players attaining a higher
standard together is to make for sterner, hard-fought
contests where, understandably, neither side dare give too
much away. Here lies the biggest change in sport and I

have followed the gradual, almost imperceptible change during my career.

Thirty years ago an English soccer side would have thought only in terms of creating and scoring goals. The two full backs, with support from a centre half, had to man the defence. Since then the best teams have been built round a disciplined, well-organized defence.

Rugby football, in the same way, used to be involved principally with attacking and pushing forward, but now balances defence and attack. So one could go on, with cricket no exception. The batsman used to get on with it, bowlers got through twenty-three overs an hour and bowled to get wickets, giving barely a thought for defence. Now he is a very poor commander in the field who does not adjust his attack, deploy his defences with each new batsman, and take into account each type of situation.

This is the fun of it and yet I have to concede how much better games would be if we attacked all the time. In my early days with Kent we never defended in the field; our bowlers would not have known how to do so. Take D. V. P. Wright, our England leg-spinner and spearhead. I sincerely believe that throughout his whole career he never bowled a ball with defence in mind. Each time he ran up to bowl he looked to get the batsman out. This is not so today. Sadly, there is, in so many matches, more defensive play from both sides than there is offensive.

There is no doubt that this new approach on the part of the players has disenchanted the cricketing public world wide and provided the seed bed for the one-day game to germinate. True, economics has played a big part too, for in the early sixties the English domestic game was losing money. Each cricketing county could not see their way clearly as to the future of the game financially. Rothman's Sunday

Cavaliers and the Gillette Cup proved the successful pathfinders, sounding the public reaction. The 60-over Gillette Cup has become an established part of the cricket calendar. The 40-over John Player Sunday League has taken over the embryo which the Cavaliers pioneered. Now the 50-over Benson & Hedges Cup has been established— another highly successful one-day competition with a slightly different format. The Prudential feature three one-day Test matches at the conclusion of the traditional series and here again this has proved itself.

Why the special appeal of one-day cricket? The public know they will see a result in a day, both sides moving forward in an endeavour to snatch victory. There is cut and thrust, continuous action, which provides good material for a television package. Moreover, it has converted millions who hitherto tended to regard cricket as some ancient English rite, clothed in a mystique and quite beyond them—now they can follow it and be caught up in it. This can only be healthy for the game, and the players, too. Moreover, the comfort of the sponsors' money has assured the future at a time when it was most needed.

So, as I look ahead, I am confident, extremely confident. The game is being watched and played by more people than ever before.

Having said that, I am concerned about the schoolboy. The cost of equipment—and cricket demands a bat, pads, gloves, boots, balls, apart from clothing—is getting beyond the reach of the average family. The father of two boys would rather they fell for football, squash, swimming or athletics than cricket—unless he was fond of cricket himself and was content to make this sacrifice.

Also, the summer examinations, now held in June rather than July, curtail the cricket season in so many schools.

However hard the National Cricket Association formulate plans to help headmasters with the various problems of cricket in the schools, such as preparing pitches, providing adequate coaching, they cannot overcome the examination hurdle. They can only look into the possibility of encouraging schools to embark on cricket programmes for youngsters after the exams, and this will mean using some of the summer holiday. Not easy, but for cricket's sake, I hope there will be cricket-loving headmasters who will be sympathetic to the idea.

Village cricket and club cricket will go on for ever, I am sure, and club cricket is receiving a fresh impetus from the local League competitions. Naturally, some resent the competitiveness of League cricket, but, presumably, they can, if they so wish, choose a club which has stayed outside it.

In the first-class game we have a mixed, well-varied balance of competitions that I have outlined. The one-day cricket has brought about newer and more athletic fielding, sharper running between the wickets and has instilled into a number of dour batsmen a confidence to take more calculated risks and to hit the ball harder. On the debit side the bowlers are learning more tricks in the field of defensive bowling—and the poor spinner is getting less and less opportunity. This spells disaster.

The slow spinner makes the game of cricket complete. He is fun to watch (I think of Bedi and Gibbs weaving their spells) and it is fun watching batsmen trying to find an answer, each in his own way.

It is no exaggeration to declare that we are in danger of losing the spinner altogether. Various things have contributed—grassier wickets, cricket balls boasting a tougher seam which retain their shine longer and, in recent years, one-day cricket, which has made their lot even more formidable. In the forty-over match they tend to become victims to the slaughter for the sloggers—and their so-called art is devalued.

Slow bowling *is* an art which can only flower and flourish in the context of a longer game where the spinner has time to buy his wickets.

The ratio of seam bowling to spin is about four to one and this must be adjusted as soon as possible.

The one-day cricket is here to stay, of course, but the traditional County game in England has to be the spinner's outlet and arena. The Bonus Points system for batting does not augur well for him either and I look for the time when our Championship game is played over four days; this would put an end to these false declarations which spoil the present three-day game. The longer the span of the game, the more demand there is for spin bowling.

The Test arena is healthy. Nowadays each one of the six countries can beat anyone else. Gone is the time when New Zealand or Pakistan might have been looked upon as the poor relations. A World Cup series would be a fascinating venture and a close-run thing. I hope it may come about.

I hope, too, that the recent movements within South Africa will lead to multi-racial sport on the cricket fields of South Africa and they—open to their African, Cape Coloured and Indian communities—can field a truly representative South African team in this World Cup.

I hope the players will be prepared to take more responsibility in cooling things down when the heat of battle on the field overspills and incites the crowds. In Test matches we must expect the spectators to be patriotic but we should guard against them becoming too nationalistic. The umpire is going to need the support and sympathy of the players if we are to achieve this. And achieve it we must, for cricket can still provide a unique platform where different peoples can meet to unite as friends. As the world grows smaller it becomes more difficult to get on with each other, it seems. We must not lose sight of the fact that within the tenets of this strange, enchanting, old game of cricket is an opportunity to create and build links, one person towards another, one school to another, one club to another, one country to another, which we would be foolish to under-estimate.

Please tackle cricket this way.

Career Details of Colin Cowdrey

Captain of Tonbridge School 1950
Captain of English Schools 1950
Captain of Oxford 1954
Captain of Kent 1957 for 15 seasons
40 400 runs in first class cricket
A Hundred Hundreds
1 000 runs in a season 26 times
113 Test Matches
Captain of England 25 times
10 Overseas Tours
7 700 runs in Tests
22 Hundreds in Tests
121 Catches in Tests